Prepare to Thrive Beyond the 9 to 5

RETIREMENT PLANNING STRATEGIES FOR YOU AND YOUR EMPLOYER

BY ANGELA WILLIAMS

Whilst the author has exercised due care and attention in the creation of this work, any statements as to the legal, financial, medical or other implications of particular actions, are made in good faith solely for general guidance and cannot be regarded as a substitute for professional advice.

ISBN 978-1-0686731-0-8

ABOUT THE AUTHOR

Angela attained membership of the CIPD (then IPM) in 1994, receiving the Jean Luck Award for the most outstanding student in her faculty. This was the start of a professional HR career that has spanned three decades.

Angela includes the leadership of a Trailblazer apprenticeship programme for the travel industry as one of her finest work accomplishments, for which she was recognised with an industry Outstanding Achievement Award.

A passionate advocate for lifelong learning, Angela gained a first-class honours degree in law through part-time study and is now working on global projects and supporting people in the late stage of their careers.

CONTENTS

INTRODUCTION

What is your life plan? Is it always to work, work, work? When you started out on your career path, did you ever contemplate a day when you would eventually stop? For many of you, the road travelled thus far may have been a bumpy one while for others, the journey may have been less eventful, but you are all arriving at this place where you have some questions and changes to confront.

In this book, I aim to support your transition from being committed to your 9 to 5 work week, or whatever guise your current work pattern has, to taking the steps required to achieve the ultimate goal of a contented and rewarding retirement.

We shall hold hands together on your journey from here, your "glidepath", sharing your experiences and working through your challenges to arrive at your new destination. Know that you are not alone, and you do possess the strength and ability to adjust to your new life beyond the 9 to 5.

"In the end, it's not the years in your life that count. It's the life in your years."

– Abraham Lincoln

1

LET THE JOURNEY BEGIN

If, like me, you have chosen to explore your options before taking this leap into the unknown, you have come to the right place. Because let's face it, voluntarily stopping work is a huge life shift. I am sure you will be okay. Why do I place such confidence in you in my opening paragraph? Well, because you are now in the great company of like-minded peers who will share strategies with you to guide you towards your goal and provide you with the necessary insights to ensure you are prepared for this next chapter of your life.

I say peers (plural) because I am not writing this book solely from personal experience, although I do draw on it greatly. I am also learning and benefiting from the experiences of others who are at various stages of their career journeys, to bring you the most appropriate suggestions and recommendations. These include colleagues and associates in my business network and friends and family members in my social sphere, as well as the best practices that leading organisations are happy to publicly share.

I write in the present tense as I am continuing this journey myself, and this book is my way to achieve self-fulfilment in my late career in tandem with serving a useful purpose in helping others. I know there is much to discover, which I believe will serve you and others well, as you learn to grow and extend your horizons outside of mainstream employment and prepare yourself for your new life ahead.

In this book, you will come across 14 keys, each one unlocking a step in your progress towards your ambition to swap your working time for more leisure time. And as you have already taken your first brave step in this journey, you have earned your very first key.

KEY #1

By acquiring this key, you have already overcome your innate resistance to making significant change – or even any change – happen in your world. Whilst some psychologists hold that humans have a fundamental discomfort with change because it disrupts the equilibrium of our cognitive and emotional states, the human body itself can affect our readiness to embrace change. Our amygdala in our brain controls the three Fs, our fright, flight or fight responses to perceived threats, and for many of us, facing what can appear to be an unknown, possibly daunting future can somehow appear threatening. Our own bodies can work against our ultimate goals and desires by creating fears that overwhelm and stop us from taking control, making plans and ultimately fulfilling our ambitions.

This frozen state of inertia is not uncommon, and with almost half of US households and over seven million people in the UK above the age of 50 not having any private retirement savings, you can count yourself as being among the more enlightened. You may have, up to now, been tempted to bury your head in the sand as the colloquial saying goes, but you have arrived at a pivotal moment in your life where you can start to take more control to shape how your future will look. You may also find that you become even better engaged with change after taking this initial step and that your progress accelerates as this new awakening takes you to places where you do, in fact, make more informed and improved choices about your future.

For many of you, this first step is the most ground-breaking and might stem from a triggering event in your life that pushes you to desire more time to accomplish some of the things you have not yet started or wish to complete. For me, it was the unexpected arrival of my granddaughter, Luna, that caused me to pause, take a breath and consider my priorities. Work was my centre of gravity, my anchor, and without it in my life, I felt I did not have an identity of my own. Luna provided me with a new purpose and caused me to question the status quo and the direction of my life, which I had not really done since my own children were born. This was a much more revealing event to me, perhaps given my age now and the stage of development of my career as opposed to when I was at a more youthful and less established position in my work-life journey.

For others, it could be a health concern, a financial windfall, a bereavement or desiring to have a strong finish in this last chapter of their working life so they may reflect overall on a positive and purposeful career journey. And yet, you don't need a reason, just a clear desire to prepare for the inevitable day your working life comes to its natural – or for some, premature – conclusion. Whatever the scenario, a mindset shift is about to begin, and to keep you focused, there are three actions I recommend you take now.

First action: Describe the aspects of your work that you believe to be your anchor or purpose.

This could be to save lives, to create investment opportunities, to make quality products, to provide advice, to support co-workers and so forth.

Second action: Describe the aspects of your life today that you believe identify your character.

You might have an outgoing nature and are involved in many activities, or you could be more insular and enjoy spending time in solitary pursuits.

Third action: Describe any changes you need to make to lessen or remove your work anchor.

You might have a calendar filled with work appointments that can be replaced with time focused on your personal wellbeing or you may have targets that can be delegated.

When the sticky elements that glue you to your job and how you see yourself as an individual are reduced to black and white, you can begin to appreciate your value and contribution to the world around you. This will be no less when work ceases to be the main feature of your life; it actually will grow even more valuable, and you can begin to shift in this more favourable direction now, at your own comfortable pace.

For men, this is especially important, as men have a lower life expectancy than women. Men born in the United States in 2023 are expected to live, on average, to age 76.9, while women are expected to live almost five years longer. In India, life expectancy for men is lower, at 65.8 years, and in the UK, the primary cause of male death is heart disease, where one in five men die before the age of 65. Heart disease is the leading cause of death globally, and a contributing factor is remaining in a high-stress environment without proper stress management techniques. I print these stark numbers to remind you that life can be short, and if you skew it towards labouring throughout your life and leaving little time in your final quartile for yourself and the things you most enjoy, can you truly say it is a life lived to the fullest?

If you really struggle to separate your identity from what you do each and every day, you need a little more time to invest in yourself, so take this time out and reflect. Don't you deserve a little focus time, a little "me-time", to discover what you're all about; what makes you who you are as a unique individual? After all, it's likely taken nearly five (or more) decades to be where you are now, and in the scheme of your life span, you have earned this right. You might be a specialist, like an accountant, a doctor, a teacher or a construction worker, or a generalist employed in retail or hospitality. Whatever your career, you are a complex individual living in a complex society with many demands on you and your time. In the next chapter, I will help you delve a little deeper into who you are as a person, what motivates you to take action and what discourages you from making the progress you need.

For now, think about the push and pull triggers in place that support a "maintain the status quo" mentality and those that encourage you to advance in the direction of your preferred date when you are free from your daily work demands.

What is Holding you back?　　　　**What is Pulling you forward?**

If you are not making progress at the rate you desire, my tip is to be truly open and honest with yourself first. Then, speak with friends, family or a trusted work confidante about your wishes so that you can begin to form intentions around your future plans.

It takes real guts to be vulnerable and share your fears – and for some, anxieties – about future uncertainties. Speaking them aloud can qualify and quantify the precise roots of the troubled thoughts that lead you to take little or no action. You are only depriving yourself when you stall and procrastinate.

Many are familiar with embarking on plans that come to nothing. Take, for instance, a diet plan started with the best of intentions, with high hopes of losing a perhaps unrealistic volume of fat in the shortest possible time, and then that tempting chocolate biscuit, when there's no one to watch, gives a very guilty sense of pleasure in that moment. What I am aiming for here is a more lasting sense of pleasure that will sustain you for the rest of your life and is therefore worthy of some investment of time on your side.

You will have formed habits in the course of your lifetime, some good and maybe some not so great. The biggest and longest-lasting habit any of you have is your work schedule, which for some may have changed considerably over the years but for others, has remained static. I am among the latter, having 30 years' employment with more or less the same employer in a professional HR role. Personally, this is the biggest life shift I face and the toughest habit to break of any that I have formed in the past, which may have included an over-reliance on chocolate and wine during certain periods of my life.

As I embark on this journey with you, I too face challenges, and I find that sharing them with you is cathartic. Perhaps you would like to do the same and share your experiences as you move through each chapter. A diary can support you as a reminder to revisit some of your incomplete thoughts and to help shape a clearer picture next time around. Whatever twists and turns your journey takes, know that others will be with you and help is closer than you may realise.

On this simple scale, I'd like you to note the importance of work in relation to your life today.

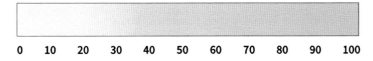

| 0 | 10 | 20 | 30 | 40 | 50 | 60 | 70 | 80 | 90 | 100 |

As you make your way through the course of this book, you will test your mind, your habits and your readiness for change. Right now, some of you might feel very far away from visualising life without your business uniform, be that your laptop, your stethoscope or your apron, and your daily commute, but gradually the very notion will become more familiar until you are ready to embrace the changes that will become your future life.

In taking this time to distinguish between your work and your identity as a person, you've earned your second key.

KEY #2

This is an important first step, so take as much time as you need to think about this distinction and keep returning to these pages to reflect upon what you've written here and where you now stand, checking the progress you are making.

2

WHO ARE YOU?

In making plans for the future, one of my preferred approaches is to check in with my peer group and seek the counsel of others who may have a different perspective that I don't readily see. As there are now four, even five generations at work at the same time, this presents both opportunities and challenges.

I thought it might be helpful to provide an overview of who these generations are, although I will concentrate primarily on the over-50s groups. And with Generation Alpha also a few years away from joining the workforce, a little knowledge of how you might interact best with each other could serve you well as you negotiate your way beyond your current sphere of reference.

See table on page 22

The Five Generations Present in our Workforce Now

1928 – 1945	1946 – 1964	1965 – 1980	1981 – 1996	1997 – 2012
Traditionalists	**Baby Boomers**	**Generation X**	**Millennials**	**Generation Z**
Most are now retired	Strong work ethic	Independent	Ambitious	Innate Tech-skilled
Loyal and hardworking	Loyal and independent	Adaptable and flexible	Tech-driven	Competitive
Face to face communications	Competitive	Informal	Personal development	Independent
Formal work environments	Results driven	Direct	Work-life balance	Entrepeneurial
Value security and stability	Focused	Technologically adept	Transparent	Positive about diversity
	Resourceful	Value work-life balance	Teamwork	Opinionated
	Process oriented		Value making an impact	Value change and new experiences
	Value teamwork			

Being mindful of these traits can help create inclusive and supportive work environments that play to the strengths of each generation. Of course, remembering that these are generalisations and with humans being human, don't expect to perfectly align to your respective category. Having a flexible and open approach when navigating intergenerational dynamics in the workplace or in your everyday encounters will yield the best outcomes.

So, as you consider your status in the overall demographical landscape of your workplace, I'd like you to explore how you may begin to see your role in passing on your knowledge and skills to the next generations. For context, I have provided a simple visual of where you might sit in the generational timeline, and I would encourage the completion of this next exercise in tandem with discussions with your peers and others from a different generational timeline.

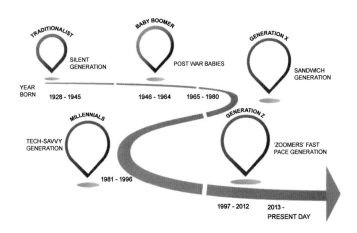

TRADITIONALISTS (1928-1945)

Picture someone who values tradition, respect and stability. They might be dressed in formal attire, like a suit, and prefer face-to-face communication in a traditional office setting. It is sometimes called the Silent Generation, as children of this generation were taught to be seen and not heard. Whilst many will be retired already, there are some whose rich knowledge of the past is waiting to be captured and shared with those who are keen to understand more about skills and practices that will otherwise soon be lost and forgotten.

Are you currently among this generation and still attending the office, even the virtual one? Setting aside your reasons for continuing with your work attendance, think about the knowledge you could share with the generations here. Many will be receptive to hearing from you, and perhaps learning how not to deal with certain matters will be just as important to them.

Action: If you are a Traditionalist, set out some of the insights you wish to share for the benefit of another generation. Note any useful feedback you receive in exchange.

BABY BOOMERS (1946-1964)

Imagine a determined individual with a focused expression, possibly in business attire, holding a briefcase. They might be surrounded by accolades or awards on their office walls. With a focus and drive to achieve results, they will generally be busy and involved in an activity with a looming deadline.

Are you among this generation? When you stop and reflect on your achievements, are you satisfied? Are you in a great place now? What advice would you give to your younger self?

Action: If you are a Baby Boomer, reflect on your answers and share your insights with those who would benefit from them. Note any useful feedback you receive in exchange.

GENERATION X (1965-1980)

Think of someone with a more casual, laid-back appearance, perhaps in jeans and a t-shirt, with a laptop or smartphone nearby. They might be in a coffee shop or co-working space, working independently but also networking with others, making the most of flexible work arrangements to get things done on the move.

Are you among this generation? What has been your greatest accomplishment? What goals do you wish to achieve before you stop working for good? Have you thought about the day you will stop working?

Action: If you belong to Generation X, consider your answers and share your insights with those who would benefit from them. Note any useful feedback you receive in exchange.

By completing and sharing your thoughts above for your identified generation, and noting the feedback received, you've earned your next key.

KEY #3

Sometimes, it is difficult to see or appreciate your true value as you come with your own biases and notions of self-worth. By having an open-mind and being receptive to helping others, you can learn more about yourself in the process. This is also an excellent way to visualise how your remaining time at work may take shape. It can serve to inform your management and your organisation on ways to maximise your potential in these later years.

I am not a philosopher, but I do trust the belief that in helping others, you do yourself a great service and open up areas of your brain that provide feel-good experiences. The neurotransmitters in your brain – such as dopamine, known as the "reward molecule" – provide a natural high when you set goals and achieve them. Serotonin, "the confidence molecule", bolsters your self-esteem and enables you to put yourself in a more vulnerable place where you may be desensitised to fears of rejection. By completing the tasks here and showing consideration towards your younger colleagues, you will not only accomplish your goals but also enhance your own self-esteem.

YOUR PERSONALITY

How ready you are to follow through with your actions may well depend on your personality type. Many organisations use psychometric tests to assess traits suitable for particular roles. I have personally used the DiSC profile to identify features of dominance, influence, steadiness and compliance (conscientiousness), but there are many others that find favour in other companies, such as the Myers-Briggs Type Indicator (MBTI), the 16 Personality Factor Questionnaire and the Neo Personality Inventory (NEO-PI) test. Psychometrics help to reveal personality types, and it is worth taking a moment to evaluate yourself to understand your strongest and less prevalent traits so that you can be better prepared to adjust to the changes that lie ahead.

I would like here to take a step back to the basics, to Carl Jung, the Swiss psychoanalyst (1875-1961) who developed the concept of archetypes, from where it could be said that modern psychometrics draw some of their inspiration. Jung's view was that all humans share a common foundation and we each build our individual experiences based on our culture, personality and life events. Our archetypes are connected with change and personal transformation.

The Archetype Circle

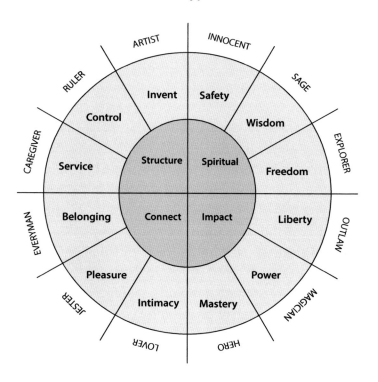

For many of you, this may be a more spiritual journey, on which you seek answers to become more informed and guide others. For others, you may seek better relationships through your connections and associations to gain new perspectives. Just as you may not represent every character trait of what typifies your generational age, you may also not exhibit just one archetype trait but display different traits at different times of your life. If you spend some time to identify your most dominant archetype, you may learn about your motivations and what holds you back to improve your self-awareness and foster personal growth.

See table on page 34

Archetype Traits

Innocent	Sage	Explorer	Outlaw
Pure, optimistic and trusting.	Wise, reflective and seeks knowledge.	Curious, adventurous and seeks new experiences.	Non-conformist, rebellious and challenges authority.
Magician	**Hero**	**Lover**	**Jester**
Mystical, transformative and possesses hidden knowledge.	Courageous, determined and willing to face challenges.	Passionate, romantic and seeks connection.	Playful, witty, unconventional and enjoys humour.
Everyman (Self)	**Caregiver**	**Ruler**	**Artist**
Relatable, adaptable, representing hidden depths of psyche.	Compassionate, nurturing and selfless.	Authoritative, responsible and organised.	Creative, innovative, imaginative and expressive.

SELF-REFLECTION

Take a moment to study the chart opposite and the descriptions. Consider times when you feel particularly aligned with these archetypes and which ones resonate the most with you. Think about how you react to good and bad times, successes and defeats, love and other life events.

Action: Note below which dominant types emerge

By knowing yourself better, you can start to identify opportunities, where appropriate, to grow and develop your more hidden traits. Where you are compliant, you may wish to follow a set agenda and not be impulsive or take risks. But it may also mean that you are not living your best life and avoiding new experiences and the benefits these bring. The saying 'strangers are simply friends who haven't met' springs to my mind when I think about venturing into a new environment that feels alien to me and where I don't know anyone – yet.

AFFIRMATIONS

If you wish to enhance a particular archetype, I recommend you be more intentional in your actions. As an example, I want to step out of my comfortable routine as I have been a creature of habit for too long. You might argue that there's nothing wrong with that, but to ready myself for the next stage of my life, where change is inevitable, I know it will be good for me to get some practice in first. Personally, I have latched onto the Explorer archetype, and having a daily affirmation, such as "I embrace my inner Explorer by trying new things", helps me to step beyond my limitations. As a bonus, it also helps me to be more creative and make new connections.

I have also been compliant, somewhat cautious and risk averse in my life, and as I find myself reflecting on the past, I know regrets are not helpful. Instead, embarking on this project is taking me into new territory and expanding my erstwhile limited horizon. If I can change, even in some small way, by being a bit more adventurous, I know that I will cope better overall.

Spend some time thinking about the archetype(s) you wish to enhance. Be intentional.

Statements such as "I embrace my inner Sage by learning from others" will hone your listening skills and help you to become more patient, and "I embrace my inner Jester by cheering other people up" will enhance your own state of mind if you tend to have a more serious disposition.

Action: List some affirmations that resonate with you and instil greater confidence in making changes to bridge gaps from your starting position to where you wish to be. It could be that you wish to be more confident, creative, brave or happy.

By completing your reflections and affirmations above, you've earned your fourth key.

KEY #4

You might wonder why you should go to this level of effort to become more self-aware when this is just a guidebook about retirement. In fact, taking some time out is a good discipline when you are so busy working day in, day out, week in, week out, repetitively, without changing your routine. You have formed habits that you need to change, and whilst some of you have time to do so before you commence your retirement glidepath, which is the time left before you reach your final working day, for others, this process needs to happen more quickly.

In the next chapter, we will look at relative perspectives on the glidepath and the practical steps you can take to move closer to your ultimate goals.

3

WHERE ARE YOU?

In this safe space, I'd like you to start thinking about that place far away in the distance that one day will be here. That place, of course, is where your mind is positioned on the day you log off from your work computer for good or you complete your last shift, signing off from the past and moving on to the start of something new. You might not be wholly clear about that something yet, but you know it will be significantly different to what you are doing today, and for many of you, what you have been doing for some considerable time. Whether you are employed, working as a contractor or have your own business, you know this day will arrive at some point, and you probably haven't really given it as much thought as you know you should. For some of you, this day is looming and for others who have more time, it's never too early to prepare for your life beyond the 9 to 5.

I am reticent about using the word "retirement" when describing your life beyond, and I use the term reservedly, as it conjures for me unhelpful stereotypical images of people with crinkled faces, white hair and walking sticks, when in fact, most people have a lot of living to experience once the paid employment regime comes to an end. Likewise, for me, the term "pensioner", whilst factually correct, does not resonate too well with my outlook, so my preference is to focus on your life beyond work as a time when you will be released from your employment commitments and be mainly at leisure to spend your time as you choose.

Of course, with more leisure time comes more opportunity to spend your money whilst your income level falls. This is a particular subject to become more educated on and around which to develop better habits and coping mechanisms in line with your new free status. As the subject of money weighs heavily upon decisions to make the break from working life, I dedicate more time to it later in Chapter 5.

To enlighten you about the road ahead, I thought it would be smart to get some first-hand knowledge of the hopes and fears that many of you may face as you approach your late career milestones and learn from these shared insights. To do this, I distributed a questionnaire (which I have shared in the Notes section) to contacts in my network to gauge their state of readiness and capture their responses. I was not surprised to note that most were not yet ready to consider stopping work, with many needing more information and support to make this transition a real event.

As men and women with young dependants have historically experienced different career paths (and I am generalising greatly here), where the mother has made the most sacrifices in career choices and career breaks to care for the children, we note that financial considerations feature more strongly in women's readiness to transition towards their life beyond. Whilst mentally, they might be more prepared to embrace the changes ahead, practical considerations may discourage them.

For men, being the hunter-gatherers – and typically the main breadwinners – deters them from stopping work as they must continue to provide for their dependants. This is a huge challenge that is not to be underestimated as it also binds men more strongly to their work-life identity than, perhaps, their female counterparts, requiring even greater effort to segregate.

Some men could heed the wise words of Dolly Parton – the composer and singer of the "9 to 5" song and star of the 1980 comedy film of the same name – who said, "Don't get so busy making a living that you forget to make a life."

Whilst acknowledging there may be certain constraints to ceasing work altogether, there are, nonetheless, steps you can take to pave the way towards a more balanced future.

HOW TO START

Whatever stage you are at in relation to your life beyond, I suggest you approach your plan in three steps, which together become your holistic programme.

Step 1: Understand Your State of Readiness

You may be ready to commit to your glidepath now, in three months or in a year's time. There may be obstacles that must first be overcome, such as family or financial dependencies or alternative work considerations. Make a clear entry in your calendar to mark your start date, the bigger and bolder, the better. Ideally, put this in full view of everyone to help you stick to your readiness timeline.

Step 2: Identify Actions You Can Implement Now

Speak with key members of your family and your colleagues to manage their future expectations. Identify habits and trends that impact your time and resources that you can begin to address. Start shifting your work-life balance.

Step 3: Close Out Any Gaps That Remain

Review and fine-tune your requirements along your journey, as you get closer to bridging the gaps from your starting position to your landing place. Are there areas you have overlooked or could not previously address due to timings or circumstances? Are you in a better place to deal with matters that were previously too onerous or out of reach?

Readiness Triangle

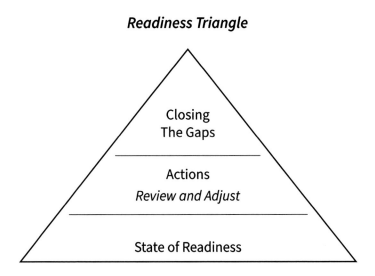

Closing
The Gaps

Actions
Review and Adjust

State of Readiness

I liken this a little to Maslow's hierarchy of needs, where you begin with capturing the security and safety of your intentions and progress to identifying and understanding your need gaps and how achievable it is to fill these in the time available. Maslow was an American psychologist whose theory was that humans fulfil their innate needs in priority order. You fulfil your physiological and safety needs first, such as food and shelter, before you meet your social needs for love and belonging, and finally, you achieve esteem and self-actualisation, where you are confident and able to reach your full potential.

Your readiness state aligns with your basic physiological survival needs in Maslow's triangle, where you need order and structure in your life. Your actions correlate with your esteem needs, where you take the necessary steps to improve and make progress with your status, and closing the gaps may be interpreted as equating to your self-actualisation or fulfilment needs when you maximise your potential and ensure that you do everything possible to secure your desired future.

Some of you might remain at or keep returning to the Actions stage and not manage to close all the gaps you desire, but embarking upon your plan in the first place is a commendable proactive place to be. Your motivation to act will be critical to making progress, and you may hit obstacles along the way that hinder you or affect your determination to follow through. And to help you move through and beyond the Actions stage, you'll want to give yourself the best chance of success, through setting SMART goals.

Whilst usually applied in a management context, there is no reason why you wouldn't set them in your personal life too. These are goals that are:

- *Specific* – for example, having a particular focus on your retirement savings, your aerobic fitness or your volunteering time. Note that it is not a general focus on your finances overall or your fitness or any charity work; you need to be more targeted to ensure you commit to your actions.

- *Measurable* – you need to be able to see your progress. It could be that you decide to move and track a retirement fund, increase your walking or running pace or allocate specific time to a chosen good cause.

- *Achievable* – there's no point in being too wild with your expectations. Small steps are more encouraging. When you achieve them, you can set new goals that build upon where you have come so far. In these examples, you could set a target of tracking the growth of your fund to a pre-determined percentage above inflation before you decide to take any action, or that you recover at a faster rate from a brisk walk or that you will spend, say, three hours a week on a good cause.

- *Relevant* – there's no point in setting goals if they don't resonate with you and are not realistic. If you know you are simply not going to personally manage your retirement savings, there's no value in setting this as a goal as you will set yourself up to fail. However, you could set a goal to educate yourself more on the subject matter instead. Similarly, if physical fitness is not something you need or wish to improve, then replace it with something that will benefit you when you are no longer working. I don't believe I have yet come across a perfect human being (have you?), and I am sure you can find something that requires your attention, be that your mind, your home or even your family members.

- *Time-bound* – as the name states, you need to draw some reasonable deadlines if you are to be motivated to act and then build on your results. Avoid setting timelines that are too long and know what works best for you. I am now constructing quarterly goal timelines and revisiting them monthly. As I get closer to my life beyond, these will become monthly or even weekly goals that I will revisit multiple times to stay on track.

YOUR STATE OF READINESS

I like to visualise measurements, possibly from my early training as an R&D scientist, and I find that a simple linear gauge is enough to help me identify where I am and how far I need to go to bridge any gaps.

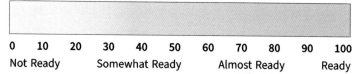

| 0 | 10 | 20 | 30 | 40 | 50 | 60 | 70 | 80 | 90 | 100 |
| Not Ready | | | Somewhat Ready | | | | Almost Ready | | | Ready |

Whilst you might not seem ready at all and might have given little thought to what you need to do to have a smooth transition to your future life, you can learn from the experiences of others and benefit from their insights. On your triangle, on page 45, your state of readiness takes up the largest area as it is the most impactful change you can make, and whilst you might have some false starts or be non-committal in your efforts, when you really are set to go, your actions will naturally follow and gain momentum.

As a starting place to help you move from your "standing still" position, I propose a 10-year plan as, in my humble opinion, the earlier you start on your readiness journey, the better shape you will be in when your chosen date finally arrives. However, I appreciate that you might be starting out later on your glidepath, so I also propose five-year and one-year timelines to cover most, if not all, scenarios.

10 YEARS TO YOUR LIFE BEYOND THE 9 TO 5

Your Financial Positioning

I suggest you start by auditing your finances, which probably feels a bit like homework – and you know how much you loved to put that off, right? But taking time out with a spreadsheet or calculator to assess your income and expenses, even the least numerate among you will be thankful for having done so.

By taking action now, you will have time to put right the areas where you may be over-reaching your budget and can narrow some of these gaps rather than allowing them to continue to grow unchecked.

If this seems like a daunting task to face alone, and if you'd rather not enlist the help of those close to you, there are specialists who can assist you for a fee. Treating this initial outlay as an investment will put you on the right track as you will have time to form good monetary habits. In contrast, if you are confident in your book-keeping powers, then there really is no excuse, is there?

See table opposite

It's simply common sense that unless your income exceeds your outgoings, allowing for contingencies, you must make changes to your current lifestyle. The act of doing so, of course, is a lot harder. Ask yourself if you really do need to make that large purchase now or if you would be better off putting the equivalent sum into your retirement savings fund. There are usually tax advantages, depending on your global location, so the more educated you become about your tax affairs, the better positioned you will be in your future life.

Financial Actions	
1. Assess your Current Situation Evaluate your financial health, your assets (savings, investments, property, other) and liabilities (loans, outgoings and commitments).	☐
2. Calculate Expenses Consider your lifestyle and estimate the expenses you'll likely need for living after you receive your final work payment (property, motoring, healthcare, travel, other interests).	☐
3. Set a Budget Construct a realistic budget. Allocate funds for essentials, savings, other outgoings and contingencies.	☐
4. Check Investments Set periodic times to review your retirement savings and adjust your fund portfolio if yields are consistently too low.	☐
5. Maximise Opportunities Increase contributions to retirement savings whenever possible such as following pay increases, bonus or other opportunities.	☐
6. Education Allocate specific times to learn about economic and regulatory impacts to your pay and retirement savings. Understand how your tax and social security deductions work. Read the financial pages of your chosen newspaper or reliable information sources.	☐
7. Reviews Keep your finances and spending under review and revisit your budget to fine-tune and re-balance your financial health.	☐

Action: Complete the checklist, above, and set yourself a SMART goal for each.

By completing your Financial Checklist with associated SMART goals, you've earned your fifth key to add to your growing collection.

KEY #5

Your Social Positioning

The importance of your social connectedness is not to be understated. By nurturing friendships and contacts and prioritising these, you may grow your social sphere to ensure you do not face your future life in isolation, without companionship or shared experiences. Loneliness is a common experience among older adults, affecting more than 10% of over 50s, and in a 2023 survey by N-IUSSP (the news magazine for the International Union for the Scientific Study of Population), in 17 out of 27 countries, the figure was as high as 25%. In the time you have before your life beyond, setting yourself some targets to store up goodwill and form new relationships will be for your greater good. Just as you did with your finances, conducting an audit of your social life, which might appear to be a strange approach, can be revelatory and help you to appreciate where you need to concentrate your efforts.

Social Actions	
1. Assess your Current Situation Evaluate your social contacts (family, friends, partner, colleagues, associates) and your activities and interests (entertainments, clubs, hobbies, sports, music, other).	☐
2. Identify Potential Growth Areas Where and when could you spend more time with individuals or groups whose company you enjoy and less money on activities that don't serve you well.	☐
3. Research Local Activities Find out what opportunities you could participate in locally. Don't exclude those you think you might not enjoy. Keep an open mind.	☐
4. Research New Activities Be adventurous. Identify a couple of areas that will bring you into contact with people who are not in your current social network.	☐
5. Give Back Identify how you could volunteer some of your time or expertise to a good cause that resonates with you.	☐

Action: Complete the checklist, above, and set yourself a SMART goal for each.

By completing your Social Actions checklist with associated SMART goals, you've earned your sixth key.

KEY #6

Your Health Positioning

Health and Wellbeing is the third focus area under your 10-year plan, and as you are starting with some time in hand, this is a great place to get your "health-house" in order. It's a common myth that establishing a new habit takes approximately three weeks, but it takes an average of 66 days for a new habit to become automatic, though that rather depends on the individual and the behaviour change that is sought. By reviewing your lifestyle choices now, you can begin to take some small steps towards adopting better habits and good practices for your future life. As this will be critical to your future happiness and sense of fulfilment, we will explore further ideas in a later chapter.

Health Actions	
1. Assess your Current Situation Evaluate your health assets (access to any private health care schemes for yourself and your family) and your own health record.	☐
2. Identify Potential Need for Treatments Where do you foresee the need for medical intervention before and after your final working day.	☐
3. Research Best Timings and Options Weigh up the costs and benefits of taking actions now or delaying them.	☐
4. Understand your Routines and Habits Be honest with yourself and note the good, the bad and the ugly with your health habits (work, exercise, nutrition, mood, other stuff).	☐
5. Record Your Progress Pay attention to your life and the triggers that affect how you are and how you act. Use journalling or other mechanisms to capture how you are changing over time.	☐

Action: Complete the checklist, above, and set yourself a SMART goal for each.

By completing your Health Actions checklist with associated SMART goals, you've earned your seventh key. You're halfway there!

KEY #7

FIVE YEARS TO YOUR LIFE BEYOND THE 9 TO 5

Being just five years out from your life beyond requires a more aggressive approach to moving from your starting position to your landing place.

5 years	2.5 years	1 year	0 years
Starting Position	Mid-way Point	Almost There	Landing Place

With less time, you need to revisit the actions above under Finances, Social and Health, and be cognisant of a new additional consideration to add to your plan, which is the potential phasing out of your workplace activities and an increase in your social presence. Where previously you may have had the luxury of more time, you must now act with renewed purpose, get done what is in your gift to do and use your best influencing skills where you are reliant upon others. At the time of writing, this is where I am on my glidepath, so I am particularly keen to share my thoughts and plans below.

Your Financial Positioning

As a woman who has had few career breaks, I am probably better placed than many of my peers who have had to stop work from time to time and break their employment history. However, I am not so out of sync with them that my finances need no attention; in fact, as the main breadwinner throughout my life, and without the best savings habits, they possibly need as much care, if not more.

To achieve the lifestyle I desire for me and my family, I have had to be more robust about using the word "no". As parents, our natural desire is to please and provide for our dependants, but being overly generous with them and putting our own future security at risk is a lose-lose outcome. Whilst our family members may yield a short-term benefit, this has a disproportionate impact if we allocate all our disposable income to their immediate demands rather than investing more wisely to make our own future more viable.

Every time you fly on an aircraft, you hear the announcement that you must put your own oxygen mask on before tending to others, and this approach ought to apply to your income too. If you are to act in a wise manner in the available work time you have left, being more self-centred and pushing more income towards your retirement plan will be in everyone's best long-term interests. Where employers offer matched contributions to retirement savings, it is a missed opportunity not to at least contribute to these maximum levels.

In tandem with becoming more protective towards your finances and curtailing your expenditure, taking time to research the best deals and opportunities for your hard-earned cash is good practice for when you will be living off your retirement savings alone.

One of the best tips I received was from a dear friend who decided in the run-up to his final working day that he would only live on the same income level that he was set to get once he had finished work. This provided him with the practice of being quite discerning about where he chose to spend his time and money and gave him the peace of mind that it was certainly achievable with some discipline and forethought. Eliminating money worries about day-to-day living gave him the impetus to move ahead without the fear of getting into financial difficulties or not being able to live his life in the way he desired.

I personally consider this a must-do experiment in the years before your final working day arrives, unless you are already set up to enjoy a comfortable financial position when your working life is complete. I can say this with confidence as, sadly, there were fewer contributors who ticked this box on my questionnaire so presumably most of you will benefit from some practice here.

Embarking on a programme to reduce your outgoings, say, three years before your final working day will set you on a good path towards managing your financial health in the long term. In particular, as you begin to reduce your working time and increase your leisure time, your income will fall, forcing you to make compromises and get financially fit.

I want you to take a short pause here and ask yourself three questions:

1. What is stopping me from commencing this experiment?

2. How can I manoeuvre my resources to move closer to a start date for this experiment?

3. When will I commit to starting this experiment?

I hope this prompts you to make some early decisions about your finances and liabilities or at least clarifies for you if and when you will be ready to commit to a scaled-back living budget.

Your Social Positioning

As with your finances, you need to also be discerning with your social activities and take a streamlined approach in deciding who and what serves you best. As your income is likely to fall, you need to avoid consistently spending money on the days you are not occupied by work. Spending time with people who will happily sit with a cup of tea or glass of wine in your home and put the world to rights with you is just as fun and productive as meeting up in a coffee shop or wine bar – but is significantly lower in cost.

Your social life is important, and you need to be able to satisfy your sense of belonging, probably even more so now, as you move towards your life beyond. Cutting back in some ways will help you financially, but the value of remaining active is also essential, and you ought not to excessively tighten your belt here when savings can be made in other ways.

A tip that I also picked up is to find out who in your social network will be available when you find yourself with free time. When you are working, it can be a challenge to squeeze time into your busy calendar to catch up, often to the disappointment of a family member or friend. You don't want to experience the reverse scenario where you are always available but those in your social network are too busy to meet up with you. This was the example provided by an individual who checked out early from their career, in advance of their friends. After an initial period of relaxation, then being busy with projects in the garden and around the house, he went back to work as he felt life was too boring and disappointing without any company to enjoy it with.

So do check that you will be sufficiently occupied after the initial honeymoon period of rest and relaxation has passed and identify ways in which you will be fulfilled. If this is not likely, then perhaps you may need to postpone your transition until such time as you know you will be in good company when you eventually do. Alternatively, seeing this as an opportunity for a new venture can be most rewarding. You may have spent so much time focusing on your career, scaling the ladder of success in your chosen field, that you became blind to alternative avenues in which your suppressed creative and entrepreneurial talents can now be realised. You see encouraging success stories of new cottage industries developed from the concepts formed in the mature brains of people in their later years, which wiser employers will do well to harness before these people disappear from their payrolls. For me, personally, this is an enlightening period where I am discovering the joys of writing, and I anticipate this being an ongoing activity throughout my glidepath and beyond.

Your Health Positioning

It's often said that "your health is your wealth", and if you don't care for yourself in the right way, you can have all the riches in the world but you won't be able to enjoy them if you are not well enough. Conversely, you may be financially wanting but have the capacity to earn more if you are fit and healthy. So I have selected a couple of housekeeping tasks for you to become more "health-savvy" in this lead-up time to your final day.

If you've been putting off seeking treatment for any health matters that your employer's health insurance may cover, now really is the time to escalate and get the treatment you need before it becomes a financial matter for you to deal with on your own. Whilst your company accountant might frown at me for making such a suggestion that will impact the cost of future policies, I remain unapologetic if it means more of you are in a fitter place when you receive your final salary payment.

In fact, now is a great time also to seek support from your employer in other ways and check what health benefits they might continue to provide for you upon reaching your life beyond.

Certain benefits, such as access to an Employee's Assistance Programme (EAP), which provides counselling services on matters like bereavement, finance, health and legal rights, could well be extended at relatively little cost to include retired employees forming the equivalent of an alumni network with their employer. Maintaining fitness through discounted gym membership or goods such as exercise equipment could also be considered.

If none are currently provided, this gives some leeway for relevant departments to try to procure them at the time of their renewal as for most organisations, this will be an annual or bi-annual exercise.

This is the time to raise a voice and seek to influence organisational policies on the type of support that could benefit you as you transition off your glidepath. The greater the demand, the increased likelihood that providers of corporate benefits will extend their offerings to include alumni members. This is definitely a focus area for me, and I'd like to think for you too now, especially if you are in a position to have a positive impact.

ONE YEAR TO YOUR LIFE BEYOND THE 9 TO 5

It's crunch time. With only 12 months remaining, the countdown clock is primed, and this is where you really need to focus on closing your gaps.

I appreciate it all sounds so simple on paper, and that those of you who have taken the time to prepare to get to this stage will have built a good foundation to set you up for a smooth launch into your future life. However, if you are coming to this realisation now and have not had any time or inclination to plan or set yourself goals, you can still achieve a smooth exit from work, albeit in a fast-track manner.

Your Financial Positioning

Understanding your tax and social security systems is especially important as you navigate this last year of receiving what will be your highest earnings (unless you derive similar or better income from other sources in the future). Taking the time to educate yourself on the most tax-efficient ways to draw your income and how to benefit in subsequent years with lower earnings is strongly advisable. This could mean that ploughing as much capital as possible into your retirement savings is your best strategy, although the time for realising your investments has now caught up with you. As some tax systems permit back-dating contributions to previous tax years, it could be a very worthwhile approach, particularly if you have spare funds, and there are tax advantages in doing so.

A note of caution on different systems, as some countries operate different ages for drawing down retirement savings, and if you are reliant upon state-funded payments too, where these are available, you need to be diligent with your research. Take this example from Europe, where an individual from France worked in Denmark for 15 years and then returned to France for her life beyond. When she turned 62, the age in France when she became entitled to receive her government-regulated payment, she only received the French part and had to wait until age 67 to receive the Danish part, meaning she had to survive rather than thrive for five years.

Many of you likely wish to achieve your life beyond without waiting for a government payment, where the trend is to keep pushing that date further and further from your reach, and, being conscious that not every person around the globe will receive such support, you must make the best of the savings you have built up for your future life through your own private arrangements and your employer's scheme. If you use this time constructively to live within the means that you will have in your subsequent years, this will certainly be one of the bigger gaps you can close on your readiness triangle.

This is also the time to implement decisions about other assets you may have, such as any property you might own and how you may be released from liabilities such as mortgages and other loans and charges. Chapter 5, All About Your Finances, focuses more closely on this.

Many of you, particularly those in Generation X, are the so-called "sandwich generation". You may have both elderly relations and younger offspring who continue to draw on your time and resources.

Young   Elderly

Whilst not wishing to sound morbid, it is also a good time, if you've not already done so, to set up the appropriate protocols, such as a Power of Attorney, to make decisions on behalf of elderly dependants, and for you too when you might need support in relation to your health and finances. A Power of Attorney is best sought while you are in good health and have full possession of your wits so you can make sound judgements about who will best serve your interests when you might be too frail to do so for yourself.

Likewise, ensuring you have a valid Will in place – so your dependants don't have to face difficult decisions alone or wait for due process to determine who the beneficiaries of your estate should be and what they should have – is a really positive step you can take now, as you put your financial house in order. There are sometimes specific promotions from lawyers who write wills for a nominal fee or a charitable donation, and the process therefore need not be expensive or complex. You are likely to have more onerous hoops to jump through if you leave these matters until you might not be in such a great place to deal with them.

Finally, as you face these final months ahead of receiving your final pay and benefit statements, ensuring that you have all your records intact for any future compliance audits is also time well spent. Adding your beneficiaries to any potential benefits, such as life assurance policies and retirement savings accounts, will also provide administrative clarity for anyone who may need to refer to them in the future.

Your Social Positioning

Don't be surprised if work interactions actually increase in this last year as you make fervent attempts to clear the decks and pass on your accumulated knowledge and records to your successors. Whilst you may have invested a huge amount of time and loyalty to your position, this might not reflect the current or future thinking of your employer in relation to backfilling your role in the same way or at all. None of us want to be remembered from a legacy work perspective like actor Jack Nicholson's character in the film "*About Schmidt*", whose wisdom and work practices were rejected by his younger successor. So, it's important that you don't prescribe too rigidly how things ought to be left or conducted once you are no longer in post.

You therefore must allow yourself time for social wellbeing in this run-up to your life beyond and not fall into the trap of being too busy doing the stuff you've always done, which won't necessarily be to anyone's overall benefit. If you've not already joined up to a local club or event to socialise regularly, you ought to try. Leaving everything to the last minute might be ok if you are definitely committed to following through with your plans, but a better approach might be to have already established some routines and connections and to have trialled a few options so that you already know where to spend your subscriptions that return the best enjoyment value for you.

Using this time constructively to identify where you might want to support your local community is also to your advantage, and if you are already reducing your working time, you can possibly increase your volunteering hours in tandem. The charity sector relies heavily on volunteers, and many receive only public support from fund-raising efforts to survive and provide much-needed services that you might expect governments to finance or subsidise. I find it intriguing how many of these good causes manage to operate solely on goodwill, and we would all be much worse off without them. I think it is a must-do experience for you to at least try to discover one worthy cause that resonates with you and lend a hand. From my observations, this practice tends to lead to even better social ties and commitments that can enrich your daily life.

Your Health Positioning

I consider your social and health positioning to be closely tied, so they complement each other. One of the most important tips I received was from people who have already come to the end of their careers and have been retired for some time. Without having a weekly structure in place – just as you have today, whether you work shifts, weekdays or weekends – every day becomes the same in effect. It might feel great that every day feels like a Saturday for those working in a conventional way, but you soon lose sight of whether today is, in fact, a Wednesday or a Friday. This can lead to confusion and affect your mental alertness and wellbeing. One day can become indistinguishable from the next and result in you missing important events and milestones.

A structured week is therefore paramount to your future happiness and can ensure you have a purpose to spring from your bed each morning. If you don't have a reason to rise from your bed, you need to invent one, whether that's household chores to be done, meeting a friend or walking an elderly neighbour's dog, for instance. Being consistent and forming routines will support your ability to lead an active life, manage your finances better and cope with contingencies or unexpected occurrences. It will also give you confidence in your social interactions where you are better placed to set and achieve your personal goals.

In this final year of work, building a framework for when you have these additional 40 hours (or however many your current workload takes up every week) will probably be one of the better ways you can prepare for your future life.

On your last day of work, when you reflect on your past and know you have done everything you could foresee and make happen, you can, with a very satisfying click, exit the door to your new life beyond, that is awaiting your imprint.

If you have managed to close these gaps in your Financial, Social and Health positioning, you've earned your eighth key.

KEY #8

4
HOW CAN
ORGANISATIONS HELP?

In Chapter 2, you faced your difficulties in taking that first step to form a plan for your future life. By sharing your concerns, I suggest that you are, in fact, breaking down the walls of silence that surround this subject in your workplace. I'm calling it "the last workplace taboo", as it is not typically an open subject for discussion amongst colleagues and management. As you begin to shine a light on the possibilities of what your organisation can do to support this transition, you can address this reticence to speak up, honestly, about your intentions.

If you are an employer, there is much that can be done to mobilise and prepare for the next generations whilst supporting your mature workforce on their glidepath. Progressive organisations are alert to the value of having formalised programmes that elicit the positive attributes of their senior workers to benefit their less experienced colleagues.

Perhaps it's my tenure and seniority that provided me with the confidence to approach my leadership team and propose what I saw as a win-win outcome to implement my own personal glidepath. Operating at a senior level within my organisation for some twenty-plus years provided me with insights that have helped me share my vision for colleagues in a similar place. I have spent a lot of my time, as do others today, attracting the brightest talents to join our organisation, and we have a wealth of materials and resources to support our approach to foster the "next, next generation", which our private shareholder remains passionate about.

What I aim for in my transition to my glidepath is to build a new and stronger awareness amongst our mature colleagues who might openly discuss ideas about their futures whilst in their formative stage and not feel obliged to follow through with them if they happen to change their minds. Indeed, if they wish to continue to be considered for promotion in the time they have remaining, this is important in the interests of transparency and fairness.

One of the key areas for exploration is in the job design you intend to maintain until your departure date. You might wish to reduce your working time but remain in your current role, your commitment being no less wavering simply because you desire a more managed route towards the time when you step away from your 9 to 5 work week. You may choose a different role that gives you more flexibility, where you can apply your existing skills or quickly learn and adapt to the new position. You may consider stepping down or a sideways move. Whatever decision you reach, it's important that you are able to freely discuss your ideas and options without pressure and without management drawing inferences about your expectations. Your decisions will, of course, be predicated on the availability of alternative opportunities and their timings within your employing organisation.

Discussions during the annual appraisal window or similar opportunities when organisations may schedule career conversations to support open dialogue between you and your leaders are ideal times to test reactions and advance your interests. If these windows are not already formally set up, then you must devise your own timing strategies that best match your chances for acceptance of your proposals. And just to state the obvious, a strategy that involves resigning from your position and hoping your manager will give in to your demands if you retract your resignation is not one that I would ever advocate.

My own example is to step away from my frontline responsibilities and work on global projects that have a far-reaching impact, one being the elevation of this new mindset towards our valued seniors. For me, this is an incredible opportunity to influence a new generation and leave a legacy that will benefit so many of my peers now and into the future, and I feel honoured to be trusted with this great responsibility.

For others, who might wish to approach management or other influencers to support a glidepath that is meaningful to them, I recommend, as a starting point, identifying a potential successor (if appropriate) and painting a picture of how you can best shape the future with your careful nurturing and investment of time within your preferred glidepath duration.

SUCCESSION PLANNING

Within my company, we apply a formal succession plan model, the 9-box, which we use to identify our future talents and those who might be struggling in their current positions. The original 9-box grid was introduced in the 1970s by McKinsey & Company, and just like psychometric tests, there are other models that have evolved over time which are favoured by other organisations. The fact that employers recognise this need is already a positive endorsement of the value placed on current members and the desire to identify successors who will be outstanding and lead their organisations into the future. Equally important is the recognition that not everyone is ambitious to fill the top roles in a business. Many have the ambition and passion to do a job well and be valued for their individual contributions.

9-Box Grid

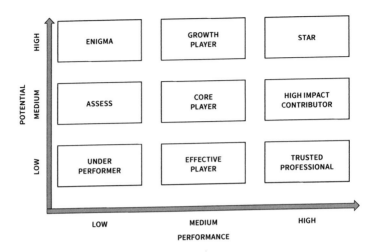

In this simple grid, you can see how you might fit into one of the spaces and what that possibly means for your successor.

The Enigma is a high-potential, low-performing person, possibly due to being new to the position or not being suited to their specific role.

The Trusted Professional is the opposite; they perform at their peak with no real need for them to progress any further from an individual or organisational standpoint.

The Core Player is the real heart and soul of a business. The majority of employees who perform solidly are Core Players.

The Star is a future leader, ready now to be promoted to the next level or higher.

There are shades in between these roles for people with higher potential or lower contributions, requiring further assessment and coaching.

The High Impact Contributor and *The Growth Employee* are people who could either expand their current roles or move higher in the organisation through targeted coaching and development.

The Effective Employee is someone who performs consistently in line with expectations and is valued for their skills and knowledge but does not demonstrate any particular leadership or expert qualities.

People in the *Under Performer* or *Assess* positions are not performing as expected and require coaching to help them succeed in their current role or perhaps a different one.

Take a few moments to study the grid and try to match yourself to the nearest description. You might consider yourself to be high potential but not achieving the performance measurements desired for a promotion, or you might be excelling but feel you are not getting the recognition you deserve for your contributions, or you might be somewhere in between.

Try to repeat this exercise through another lens –
maybe how you think your manager or colleagues
might view you. Would they say you are always in
a rush to get things done and move on to the next
challenge, or are you more relaxed and like to take
things slowly and steadily? Would they describe you
as knowledgeable, expert even, and in a comfortable
place in your career, or would they say you have a lot
to learn and are very ambitious? Might they think of
you in other ways?

Action: With these thoughts in mind, note who could be your closest successor. What are their attributes and skills?

Note that they might not exist in your organisation today, or they could be at a different level or from an alternative functional or geographical area.

It might be the case that a successor cannot be identified, or might not even be required, to support your glidepath, but this is an important first step to preparing your exit strategy and supporting your management and colleagues for the new future that also awaits them.

Identifying successors is not the only piece of the jigsaw puzzle that employers must gauge in order to plug the gap of the departing older workforce, and this is where tapping into these talents can make a significant difference in the preparedness of the organisation to let this experience go.

By completing your succession plan, you've earned your ninth key.

KEY #9

BUILDING A MENTORING PROGRAMME

Mentoring is akin to coaching; however, there are subtle differences, which I will explain for clarity. Mentoring involves a more experienced person (mentor) sharing their wisdom and insights with a less experienced individual (mentee) with the mentor's expertise forming a significant part of this relationship. The mentor is also a guide for the mentee in their broader life and career aspirations and tends to form a nurturing and enduring relationship. Coaching, on the other hand, is more formal and tends to be for attaining specific goals in a defined period of time with the coach offering guidance and feedback to the coachee.

There are many mentoring platforms and models, and you need to identify which is best for you and your organisation. They range from traditional one-to-one programmes, where one mentor is paired with one mentee, to group mentoring with one or more mentors facilitating multiple mentees. Peer mentoring, where colleagues at a similar level share knowledge and experiences, can be mutually beneficial. Reverse mentoring is where a younger or less-experienced individual mentors older and more experienced workers.

Career mentoring is where the mentor guides the mentee in their development and advancement. Speed mentoring is where the mentee is allocated a specific time to seek answers from their mentor to questions they have prepared. I liken this to speed-dating, and it can be effective where there is limited time available to ensure mentoring is productive.

Mentoring can be virtual or in person, and both formal and informal approaches exist. Mosaic mentoring is a concept where the mentee may benefit from multiple mentoring strategies at the same time, so they could, for instance, have informal mentoring with one mentor and a more formal approach with another whilst belonging to a group mentoring programme and engaging in speed mentoring practices.

My preference is to have a hybrid approach, to operate a formal structure but have much informality between the mentor and mentee to determine what works for them in relation to purpose, timings, locations and regularity of connections.

Mentoring Models

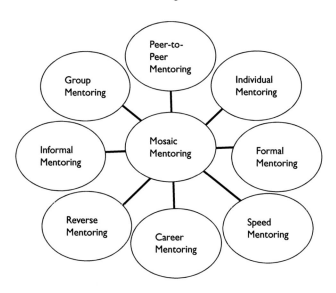

As the goal is to retain within the organisation the knowledge held by your mature colleagues, a good first step in establishing a mentoring programme is to conduct a talent mapping exercise. It will be the basis for teaming up mentors with the right skills and experiences to the relevant mentees who will benefit most. This centres on the critical and scarce skills required for the future and ensures the mentoring programme is a valuable and dynamic resource that evolves as the business and the world around us change.

As you highlight the critical roles and skills that impact your business outcomes the greatest, you can determine the necessary attributes sought in the people you might identify to fill them. With your current talent known to you, you are able to draw a baseline of current competence and where gaps need to be bridged to achieve your ultimate organisational goals.

If your company does not have digital technologies to conduct skills mapping exercises, a simple grid matrix in a spreadsheet can help you log these requirements, and there are many templates online to support your business requirements, such as the example here:

Critical Skills Mapping Chart					
	Worker 1		Worker 2		Worker 3	
SKILLS	Current Expertise	Growth Potential	Current Expertise	Growth Potential	Current Expertise	Growth Potential
Public Speaking	2	3	3	3	1	1
Commercial Acuity	2	2	2	3	2	2
Creative Application	2	1	1	1	2	2
Digital Proficiency	1	2	2	1	3	2
Leadership Strength	3	3	2	1	1	1
Written Communication	3	3	2	2	3	2

Expertise: 3= Expert, 2= Competent, 1= Significant Skills Gaps

Growth Potential: 3= High Potential, 2= Moderate Potential, 1= Limited Potential

Using your talent mapping insights, you can design a curriculum with learning outcomes for the mentee. This will provide structure and meaning for you as a mentor so that sessions together will be targeted and productive. As time is precious for both parties, this will also lead to more impactful knowledge transfer from the mentor and retention by the mentee. Opportunities to learn from mentors, through personalised development plans and stretch assignments – where the mentee is given wider exposure to business areas they will need in the future – are highly rewarding and have mutual benefits. The mentee gets to spend time with a nominated mentor whom they might not otherwise ever meet or gain valuable insights from, and the mentor is fulfilled by passing on wisdom and know-how to inspire other members and newer generations.

In tandem with the mentoring model development, growing a mentoring network is necessary to broadly share expertise and learning across the generations. You know that you are uniquely placed with potentially five generations sharing the same workspace at the same time, and understanding how these generations interact and what is their preferred modus operandi is crucial to a successful programme. It will ensure that you surface the advantages and mitigate any shortcomings or conflicts that could potentially arise with the competing priorities of these generations. A strong match between the mentor and mentee is powerful and desirable, so when there are few synergies, you must be ready to make the necessary tweaks and switches to ensure the correct mentee is placed with the most suitable mentor.

Honest, constructive feedback is essential to make the necessary improvements on a continuous basis. Giving feedback to an older, more senior worker may prove challenging for some, and as a mentor, you should be aware of times when your mentee might struggle to voice their true feelings. Whilst it might not be what you want to hear, to support the overall veracity of the programme, feedback is to be encouraged. Educating your mentee on how best to provide you with feedback is important. Whilst some people in their personal relationships might have informal ways, such as choosing an agreed "safe" word when they are about to come clean about something, I propose you choose the STAR method or a similar feedback method:

Star Feedback Model

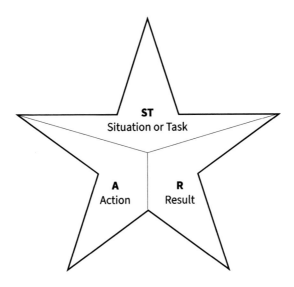

By speaking about the situation (S) and/or task (T) and breaking this down into its component parts, explaining the actions (A) taken and the results (R) or outcomes, you provide a way to communicate that removes any personal bias that could prove awkward or even upsetting to more sensitive individuals. Creating a rapport and building a strong relationship that surpasses the day-to-day urgencies and priorities will have long-term benefits for all parties.

A robust mentoring programme is therefore integral to the whole talent life cycle of the organisation, taking into account the entire employee experience from the skills and knowledge that may be enhanced for the new recruit, to the employee whose performance requires improvement, to those ready for a transfer or promotion to a new position.

The connections between you as a mentor and your mentee are multiple, and you may find these experiences open up further ways to influence how your succession may evolve. As my line manager would often say, "It's an evolution, not a revolution," and your nurturing and encouragement of these skill sets, mean you continue to be an essential and relevant resource in the future management toolkit.

With this proactive preparation, you can achieve, calmly and intelligently, the desired succession outcomes to be able to start your life beyond with a clear conscience. Here, I'd like to give a shout-out to all mentors who patiently and generously pass on their wisdom and knowledge and to organisations who embrace and invest in this transition towards a smoother continuity of leadership and expertise.

According to a 2024 survey, the median profits of Fortune 500 companies with mentoring programmes in the US were more than double those of companies without. Yes, you heard that correctly: x2, double! So it not only makes practical and common sense but it is also a sound commercial basis for companies to embark on this journey with those of you on your glidepath. One such company to achieve this impressive yield is the French company, Sodexo, a global leader in sustainable food and facilities management services, through their Spirit of Mentoring programme. With both informal and formal mentoring approaches, silos across divisions and departments were eliminated and a more engaged and confident workforce emerged. Cross-cultural and networking connections improved, along with the skills growth and job prospects of the overall workforce. Named repeatedly on Fortune's *"World's Most Admired Companies"* list, Sodexo stands out as an impressive organisation that has embraced and directly benefited from corporate mentoring approaches.

ALUMNI

I've chosen "alumni" for want of a better term, but I feel it captures what organisations can offer to support you as you transition off your mainstream employment path. For many of you long-tenured workers, leaving behind a lifetime of work – with memories of the highs and lows and colleagues who have become firm friends and akin to family – is a very definitive change that you might otherwise never be ready to accept.

If your organisation facilitates a continued relationship with you as you commence your life beyond, there will be multiple benefits. Not least, it will enable you to commit to a glidepath deadline, knowing that you can still connect with the people who have mattered and continue to be important to you. It will also keep you around for those all-important questions that only you can answer due to your history and inside knowledge. Additionally, it will provide the certainty and security your employer wants as the organisation moves forward with your successors, especially in the early stages of your life beyond.

An alumni community of ex-colleagues and associates is a rich source of talent that can also be put to great use on a volunteering basis. Members willingly provide support to good causes that the organisation supports in local communities and can add value to committees where a variety of views and opinions are sought. Being a step away from the business can lend itself to a more independent and honest appraisal of what improvements are best and how to bring them about. Whilst members also benefit from social engagement and a continued sense of belonging within business communities, participation can also be highly valuable from a health and wellbeing perspective.

With little or no expense required for the creation of an alumni community, as these tend to be mainly run and managed by interested parties already starting their new life chapter, I recommend making this part of the normal offboarding process for workers reaching the end of their careers.

The benefits, I believe, speak for themselves.

GOVERNMENT/REGULATORY CONSIDERATIONS

The Pew Research Centre reports that in the US, the older workforce has nearly quadrupled in size since the 1980s. On the opposite side of the globe, we have the oldest workforces worldwide in Japan, South Korea and New Zealand, according to the 2023 Pensions at a Glance study by the OECD (Organisation for Economic Cooperation and Development). Iceland, New Zealand and Japan, also host more employees above the age of 55 in their workforce demographics, with Sweden and Norway following closely, compared to other OECD member countries. The proportion of the world population aged 60 or older has more than tripled since 1950, with 1 in 10 in this age bracket, and will almost triple again by 2050, with 1 in 5 in the over-60 cohort.

Proportion of the world population aged 60 years or older

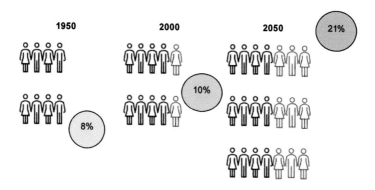

What does this mean for older workers? Policy initiatives such as establishing "Silver Human Resource Centres" in Japan and introducing the Retirement and Re-employment Act in Singapore, as well as trends across the globe to raise the age before eligible citizens can access retirement benefits, all serve to encourage retention in work of our older workers.

Programs like Snowbird in the US help older employees to shuttle between a warmer climate during the cold winter months and a cooler climate in the summer months, with the retail and hospitality sectors particularly benefiting as their customer base also tends to migrate in these directions. In the Netherlands, initiatives like the Silver Starter Service for the over-50s provide education for entrepreneurs to help transform their ideas into their new business ventures, and Senior2go brings senior entrepreneurs together to collaborate and develop products and services.

Action: Consider whether it is a good thing to maintain employment in later life, what support is provided by government institutions where you live and record your thoughts.

Where do I stand on this particular topic? I see both pros and cons. There are financial benefits, and potential health benefits too, for older workers who remain in employment. Shifting the onus back to employing organisations to retain an ageing workforce delays our exit, which, in turn, can block aspiring talents who may leave organisations to seek promotions and opportunities elsewhere.

A solution that I advocate is for governments around the world to offer tangible financial contributions in the form of tax breaks or similar mechanisms to help employers manage these important competing dynamics; retaining an older workforce whilst encouraging younger generations to scale the corporate ladder. Supporting the interests of older workers through better-funded retirement savings provision during their working lives must be a better proposition than continuously pushing further out of reach, the statutory age when eligible citizens become entitled to a state-funded income, leading to enforced longer work-lives than might be desired.

The OECD reported in 2023 that three-fifths of its member countries were set to increase their normal retirement ages, and this is a trend that doesn't look like it will ever be reversed. Indeed, given our world demographics, it is perhaps just a matter of time until more state-funded superannuation schemes adjust to means-based tests rather than be seen as an entitlement based on lifetime contributions.

The encouragement of better long-term savings and investment strategies for younger workers, such as compulsory retirement contributions as a percentage of every employment undertaken, would be one way to prevent poverty in old age and enforced longer working lives.

AGE Platform Europe's 2023 Barometer proposes an employment rate of 78% for those aged 20 to 64 by 2030. In some countries, such as Greece and Romania, the retention of women in employment between the ages of 55 and 64 is way below, at a lamentable rate of less than 40%. The report found that two-fifths of people aged between 55 and 64 are not in work and that long-term unemployment (more than 12 months) is higher for older workers.

This is contrary to what we desire for our senior workers who have a lot to offer employing organisations, as we have seen with Fortune 500 ROI outcomes, and rather than curtailing their careers prematurely and never giving them the opportunity to choose how to gracefully exit work, a positive growth mindset is to be encouraged towards our older workers.

Placing the burden of supporting the elderly squarely on employers' or taxpayers' shoulders is not the only approach that governments can take, and I believe a hybrid of the two to be more sustainable. Whilst countries like Singapore, with their Senior Worker

Support Package, offer employers grants and tax incentives to re-employ older workers on a flexible and part-time basis, they are among the few who do. And for countries that have no such provision for their citizens, with many having just a basic or means-tested social security infrastructure, this will continue to promote a conflicting dynamic between employers' requirements and workers' and citizens' rights and desires.

LEGAL MATTERS

Before we depart from our focus on how organisations and institutions may support the older workforce, it feels remiss not to mention at least some of the legal protections that you have as you mature. As a HR practitioner and law graduate, I would like to ensure you move onto the next phase of your working life aware of your rights and the obligations of your employer and those you may serve. Whilst I believe most people and organisations act in good faith and would aim to fulfil your glidepath requirements, recognising any shortcomings that are not in your best interests will enable you to raise your concerns in a constructive manner and achieve a more favourable outcome.

Treating an older worker less favourably than another person may amount to a breach of human rights, and in many jurisdictions, there is legislation on age discrimination to protect against unfavourable treatment, such as the Age Discrimination in Employment Act (ADEA) in the US, the Ontario Human Rights Code in Canada and The Equality Act in the UK. Members of the European Union benefit from the Employment Equality Directive that makes age discrimination unlawful, and the United Nations also promotes older persons as "rights bearers" to guarantee dignity and equality throughout their lives.

Not applying an equal opportunities policy fairly and passing an older worker over for promotion, demoting them, selecting them for redundancy or treating them in other adverse ways will be discriminatory if age is a factor in any such decisions. There might be justifications for some discriminatory practices, if it is a proportionate means of achieving a legitimate aim. European legislation currently permits this approach in certain cases, so, for example, if an employer sets a compulsory termination date for all workers reaching a specific retirement age, this will be permitted if it is strictly applied, is needed for workforce planning and can thus be objectively justified.

Sometimes, discrimination can be unintentional. An interviewer might select younger favourable candidates in their likeness – the so-called "halo" effect – and not even be aware of doing so. To alter the course of an individual's future adversely, through a lack of awareness or due care, is simply not acceptable in today's workplace.

As you embark on your glidepath, your employer needs to be cognisant of their actions in case they could be misconstrued, simply because you have been open and transparent with your exit strategy or that you are getting older. Training and guidance for the whole workforce on how to behave without bias towards each other is strongly advocated, particularly for management and those in decision-making roles.

Employers must also provide a healthy and safe workplace for all staff, regardless of age. With many musculoskeletal conditions arising from poor posture at workstations, risk assessments become even more important for the older employee who may have a sedentary role – working virtually, out of day-to-day sight of others – and who experience age-related bone and muscle damage. It is recommended that employers conduct an assessment annually, or more frequently for vulnerable employees, and I suggest that older workers would especially benefit from regular assessments of this type.

Recognising the particular needs of the mature workforce – who may need greater flexibility with appointments to check on their medical fitness and more frequent breaks from repetitive tasks or exertions that could give rise to strain injuries – will contribute towards discharging employers' duty of care. Making reasonable adjustments to the environment, such as improving the lighting, and providing support in job design with more time for completion of tasks will create a positive and productive age-friendly work environment.

Physical health is one area where employers have a duty of care towards employees, but mental health in particular is fast becoming a subject for greater employer attention and support. With improved awareness of some of the stresses and anxieties facing older staff, including a possible decline in mental cognition and ability to cope with modern working practices, employers have a responsibility to ensure adequate wellbeing protections are in place. Having clear, published policies, such as a specific menopause or neurodiverse policy, shows commitment from organisations towards their employees, no matter their situation or circumstances.

This is not only conducive to supporting the older workforce. It can support members of all age groups who can thrive in a workplace culture designed to be accommodating and flexible towards each person's individual needs.

5

ABOUT YOUR FINANCES

How do you tackle the thorny question of what you will need when you transition to your life beyond? In Chapter 3, you assessed your financial positioning by conducting an audit and a budgeting exercise to better understand your disposable income and how to live within these limits. In this chapter, I'd like you to take a closer look at yourself, your appetite for risk, your current and future spending habits, your retirement savings and other assets you have so that you are better placed to afford the life you desire.

You appreciate that your financial positioning plays a huge part in your readiness to move onto your glidepath, which is why I am giving it the attention it warrants. Whilst I don't have magic fairy dust to sprinkle over your bank accounts, I do wish to share information to try and put you in a more informed place from where to face your future. You know and can admit to yourself that burying your head in the sand is not helpful to increasing your wealth, yet you continue to do so and ignore the possibilities of addressing and changing your financial status. You're not alone in this, and what seems very difficult at first and incredibly daunting for many, can be liberating once you set yourself a SMART goal and start tackling what you most fear.

When I first started to look at my own finances, which were wanting in many ways as there's never really enough for what we desire, I was reminded of The Starfish Story. For anyone not familiar, this is a story originally written in 1969 by Loren Eiseley, an American anthropologist, and adapted over time. It is about an older, wise man walking along a beach strewn with millions of starfish washed up after a storm. In the distance, he spots a young lady moving like a dancer and approaches her. As he gets closer, he sees that she is picking up the starfish and very gently returning them to the ocean. He asks why she is doing this, and she explains that the sun is rising and the tide is going out and they will all die. The wise man asks what the point is when there are miles and miles of beach covered with starfish and she cannot possibly make a difference. The young lady listens respectfully, pauses and then picks up another starfish and gently returns it into the water, seeing it disappear past the surf and the breaking waves and quietly replies, "I made a difference to that one."

The old man shrugs his shoulders, hesitates and thinks. Inspired by her, he joins in, picking up a starfish and gently returning it to the ocean. Others observe what they are doing and team up to save as many starfish as they can.

I love this story. True or not, it has inspired me to do many firsts over the years and tackle the big stuff that initially appears so overwhelming, including taking my first step on my financial planning journey, which was to educate myself on my retirement savings plan and make some key changes to ensure it could better meet my needs.

As part of the route I designed towards the actualisation of my own life beyond, I recognised that my retirement savings were insufficient to provide me with the lifestyle I desired. In weighing up my choices, I approached my senior leader about my dilemma and put forward the idea of reallocating more of my pay into my retirement fund. This was to our mutual advantage, as at the time, there were lower social security thresholds to be met by my employer. Whilst this may not be an option for some, depending on our geographical positioning and regulatory controls, it is certainly an area I would advocate exploring where it is at all feasible.

RETIREMENT SAVINGS

I mentioned previously that almost half of households in the US have no retirement savings at all. Of those who have managed to save, just 17% of women and 26% of men feel like they are on track to meet their financial goals, with women having an average fund size 30% smaller than their male counterparts.

Hindsight is a wonderful thing, and if we all had it, we would undoubtedly have paid far greater attention to our retirement savings at an earlier stage of our working careers. And for any of you with younger members in your teams or family, you can do them no greater service than to help them establish sound habits in this regard. Many people spend to their income limits and beyond, and if they make contributions directly from their pay, this ensures they always grow their savings fund, whether remaining within their spending limits or not.

A general rule of thumb is to save half of your age as a percentage of your income towards retirement, so if you are 50, you should save 25% of your gross income. Whilst easier said than done, a habit formed in your youth makes this a lifetime commitment that many are grateful they adopted when reaching later milestones.

We live in a society today where instant gratification is the default expectation, whether it's with your entertainment choices and on-demand streaming of movies and music or almost instant deliveries of products and food to your doorstep. You need to have an opposite approach to your finances and build and maintain longer-term strategies that grow over time, with the patience to wait for the optimum moments to cash in or re-invest.

Your Risk Profile

Better understanding your attitude to risk will help you to navigate the plethora of options for where your hard-earned cash can grow. Your personality type provides you with clues as to how predisposed you are in this regard, and having spent a little time on this in the earlier discovery chapter about yourself, you know more about how you might react to your financial position and circumstances.

- *The Conservative* or *Cautious* amongst you naturally opt for low-risk products and prioritise the preservation of your portfolio value over maximising returns.

- *The Moderate* of you accept a balanced approach to maintaining capital assets with higher-growth returns.

- *The Aggressive* or *Adventurous* among you take higher risks for higher gains and accept higher potential losses.

Many financial publications and banking institutions (e.g. Forbes, Royal London, etc.) provide risk assessment tools to assess your propensity for risk, which I won't replicate here. I'll just highlight that they are readily available online, and using one of them is an exercise I recommend you carry out.

Action: Think about your appetite for risk and where your current savings are invested. Note them down here. Are they aligned to your risk profile? What change (if any) would you make to improve their long term growth?

Educating yourself better about your attitude to risk will support you in understanding when your expectations are mismatched, such as having a cautious approach and anticipating instant high-yield returns. By understanding your optimum exposure to risk for your own peace of mind, you may learn to diversify and apply your investment strategy accordingly. In the same way, managing your budgets and household expenses closely, and I mean to the nearest dollar or pound, which you did in Chapter 3, provides the insights you require to instil wiser spending and investment habits, in line with your disposable income and glidepath duration.

By ensuring a greater awareness of your own risk profile and taking actions accordingly, you've earned your tenth key.

KEY #10

Corporate Schemes

In some countries, such as Australia, Hong Kong, The Netherlands and the UK, it is compulsory for employers to provide a pension scheme for their employees and contribute at minimum rates set by government. Corporate retirement savings plans usually have a standard default fund, based on the risk profile of the members and the aims of the fund. Its purpose could be to provide specific or varied benefits as the members come to their life beyond, such as purchasing an insurance or annuity contract or leaving funds invested.

Management of your investments by regulated financial bodies takes the decision-making away from you with the added comfort of knowing that your capital is being invested with professional expertise and governance, which, in my experience, has worked well for employees who generally display an apathy towards such matters until the time arrives to draw upon them. Default models are designed to move from more volatile investments within equities markets to more stable and lower-risk investments in property stocks and government bonds as you near your preferred glidepath end date in order to be more shielded from stock market fluctuations.

If you are a contractor, having multiple contracts with various employing organisations throughout your career can be an inconvenience when aiming to save consistently. This is why treating your retirement savings with equal respect to your tax liabilities is essential to building your personal portfolio and ensuring you do not deprive yourself of adequate funds for when you eventually stop working.

As a guide, it is well to appreciate that for approximately every $100k in a retirement fund, if you choose to purchase an insurance contract to provide an annual income for life, this will generally give you around $5-7k income per year, depending on factors such as interest rates, underlying fund performance and your own health. In the US, the recommended guidance is to withdraw 4% of the portfolio balance for living expenses annually (although this might be falling out of favour as being too low to meet current living standards). In Singapore, an individual would need around $2.3k per month, equating to a fund of around $400k. With the average pot for US family members in 2024 being $87k, and a savings pot for women in the UK of £69k being around 25% of the recommended value for a moderate standard of living, you can see the outlook is not rosy. In sharing such realisations, my intention is not to scare but to provide a wake-up call so that you can appreciate the implications if you are not more in tune with your current and future financial status.

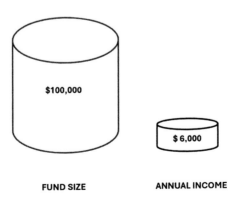

FUND SIZE   **ANNUAL INCOME**

What about those of you who did not have the means or time to put your own financial house in order? As mentioned previously, you need to take your own oxygen before you can help others, and if you have not done so up to now, you **must** do so as a matter of urgency.

Retirement savings can be a complex area where people might possibly have different savings pots with different providers in countries where there is the freedom to have these multiple investments. Tracking them down can be an arduous but essential task on your must-do checklist, particularly where providers have changed ownership. Your social security identification may support this process, and thoughts around the amalgamation of these funds whilst desired from a consolidation viewpoint, should be treated with care, especially if there are potential fees to transfer them. Understanding the charges that are applied to investments is also important, and many company-provided schemes will enjoy discounted management fees that are passed onto members.

Where companies contribute to workers' plans, it is unwise not to belong to such a scheme as ultimately, this is free money that may otherwise be lost to you. If you are not included when you ought to be, even though you may have left it pretty late in your working career, you should seriously consider enrolling, unless there is a very compelling reason not to.

Special Considerations

In regions where a state-funded income is provided, there may be an opportunity to make good any shortfall in social security contributions that could affect the value of the income to be drawn. This shortfall could arise from periods of absence from work or living abroad and is another area to research – and, if possible, rectify – if the adjusted income would make sense for such a gap to be filled. Over the years, much has been written about the career-break effects on women who have provided free childcare unburdened to the state, as opposed to forging stronger employment opportunities, and it is worth making enquiries to see if missed contributions can be backdated and what other support is available.

One of the few times when having a shorter life expectancy through poor fitness and health is beneficial is in the potential payout of a retirement savings plan based on actuarial data that includes mortality rates. Take an example in the UK where people living in Glasgow in Scotland, which is considered to have a higher mortality rate than London, would receive a higher retirement income from the same fund size as their London-based counterparts – the rationale being that the payment would be made over a shorter lifetime span and therefore could be higher. I'm not at all proposing you change your lifestyle habits to the detriment of your health, but I mention this to highlight the complexity of the multi-faceted financial position in your life beyond.

YOUR SPENDING HABITS

On your must-do list is to consider the realistic outgoings you will have as you age. Depending on your glidepath timeline, you could have another 30 years or more to eke out across your future, but the likelihood of continuing to spend at the rate you do in your 50s and 60s is likely to wane as you get to your mid-70s and beyond. Whilst you may face other challenges with medical and healthcare costs, your day-to-day spending requirements will likely be less.

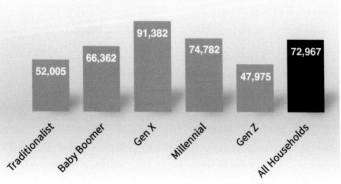

Mean household expenditure in $US

You can see that as you age, your household expenses reduce, and whilst this data comes from the US, a similar trend is seen globally.

One of the differentiators for you now is to distinguish your **needs** from your **desires**. You have spent some time already analysing your finances and producing your budget to support your goals. Now, you must allocate some thoughtful decision-making time to breaking out your spending patterns and prioritising them into what you class as:

1. Essential for survival (food, rent, utilities, medical expenses, etc.)

2. Essential for living (social, transport, health, retirement savings, etc.)

3. Everything else (entertainment, travel, other savings and investments, etc.)

Using your budget template (many are available online) in software like Excel or within your own banking apps, add a column to identify which of your outgoings fall within each of the above three categories.

Action: Consider the importance of Category 3 items and their impact on your happiness, whether High (their absence will have an adverse effect) or Neutral (they will not materially affect you).

With items that have a high impact, identify those that can wait (e.g. a new phone, another handbag, replacement furniture, etc.) and try to balance short-term desires against longer-term goals, such as growing your retirement fund. If you can prioritise your longer-term goals, making these short-term compromises now will benefit you by giving you greater spending control and power when you reach your life beyond.

By completing this exercise and building a better understanding of what's really important to you in both the short and the long-term, you've earned your eleventh key.

KEY #11

Closely inspecting all of your spending habits can highlight patterns where you overspend unintentionally and help you to be more discerning. Many of you may subscribe to multiple entertainment channels but only use a couple of them regularly, or you may pay for services that are already available free from other sources, such as travel insurance and other discounts that many banks offer their customers. My own examples include a music streaming channel I subscribed to for my children, who already had their own, and a fitness app that I downloaded and immediately forgot about that had a yearly auto-renewal that I had not spotted. Needless to say, there were no refunds, but at least they were costs I stopped incurring, and as a family, we became more vigilant to ensure we didn't get caught out again.

There might be times when, even with the best-laid plans, you struggle to make ends meet, and whilst I have tended to shy away from credit facilities for most of my life, given my own risk-averse disposition, I did benefit when my cash flow was temporarily affected. It was a time when I didn't want to access any additional borrowing, and as I knew there would be a payment due to me in the future, I opted for a credit card that permitted me to make no payments for 24 months without any interest and then pay the balance off in full, without penalty. This plugged the gap for me perfectly and is an approach I would personally use again if, for example, I did not wish to access a savings scheme that is due to pay a bonus on maturity that I would otherwise forfeit.

I'm not really sure that I am the type of customer banks wish to target for such credit facilities, but all is fair in the world of finance if we can have these occasional wins. I mention this because changing my own attitude and approach to my finances has had a surprising upside, and using a line of credit that I would never before have entertained actually improved my financial circumstances. Where once I was always loyal to my bank, I am now more inclined to switch when there are decent incentives to move, and I apply the same approach to other services I receive, including household utilities and mobile and broadband communications. I've found on many occasions that merely enquiring about moving my custom away spurred the incumbent provider to come back with better offers to retain me.

Being open to ideas that might place you outside your comfort zone can be rewarding if you do your homework well and have the means to meet your future obligations. And where you face multiple pressures on your finances, the golden rule is to protect your basic needs first in your hierarchy triangle; so your mortgage or rent has top billing, next come food and utilities and then any loans or financing that command the highest interest rates and should be paid down as quickly as possible. This ensures you prioritise repayments that are the greatest drain on your pocket whilst safeguarding your essential living requirements.

PROPERTY ASSETS

For those with property, being on your glidepath might also be the time to consider possible moves towards a lower-maintenance home and prepare your asset for sale in order to enjoy a less expensive outlook when your income is reduced. Waiting until you are older and less inclined to cope with such upheaval is procrastination that serves no good purpose. A move to a less expensive geographical location might also be worth serious consideration if your local ties are not entrenched. The same holds true if you are in rental accommodation and can benefit by moving to a lower-cost location when your tenancy is due for renewal.

As this may be a rather involved project, thoughtful care and planning are needed. A SWOT analysis (see below) can prompt you to consider all aspects before you plough ahead. It will help you to rationalise whether you are up for the challenges, whether you would be with some modifications, or whether you're not up for them at all.

STRENGTHS	**WEAKNESSES**
OPPORTUNITIES	**THREATS**

S for Strengths: These are internal factors within your control that will support your project's success. Examples could be the people you know who can advise and help you or your own expertise and motivation.

W for Weaknesses: These are internal factors that hinder your progress. Examples could be budget limitations, resources and timescales.

O for Opportunities: These are external factors that could benefit you. Examples could be the current housing market position and the availability of building materials at a reduced cost.

T for Threats: These are external factors that pose risks to you. Examples could be the economic climate or unforeseen contingencies.

You can apply the SWOT approach to many scenarios, not just to your financial standing.

If you decide that the costs and trouble outweigh the benefits, you might consider an equity release scheme instead. These schemes have become popular in recent times and could be an option if you wish to remain in your property. This is a strategy that permits a drawdown of money as a loan from the value of your home, which you do not have to repay until you leave, at which point the money with interest and charges is repaid. As there are many scams to entice away your lifetime earnings in this part of your glidepath journey, extreme care needs to be exercised before committing to such a course of action, and only do so after thorough research and with a reputable organisation.

Also worth exploring is the viability of letting a room in your property to earn extra income, which could be on a short- or long-term basis. If you have the space, you could think about becoming an Airbnb host, if you wouldn't be fazed by having different guests staying in your home from time to time. If you are in leased arrangements, check to see whether this is permitted under your tenancy agreement or whether you need to seek permission.

Some people find other novel ways of using their homes for income, such as providing car parking spaces on their driveways in urban areas near attractions or stations, where parking is limited and alternative options are some distance away or very expensive. Some may offer garden space to green-fingered enthusiasts to grow market produce and other saleable products. I came across an example where a homeowner let out a self-contained garden room for use by multiple practitioners, some carrying out hair and beauty treatments and other holistic therapies. It was a win-win for those without a fixed salon base and the owner, who received a steady income. Getting yourself on a register to let out your property to host people for national or international competitions or even television productions, whilst disruptive and short-lived, can also be lucrative.

OTHER INCOME

Some amateur endeavours that you may have as a hobby, such as home-brewing, pet care, crafts, photography, gaming and social media content creation, could provide a source of income that you might not have considered up to now. As many of you try to become more sustainable in your shopping choices, there is a trending preference for unique artisan products that support local endeavours and have a lower carbon footprint, which the more creative among you could exploit.

In my research, I came across a group of people who help each other to navigate the stock market and trade like professionals, enjoying a modest income without using their own capital to get started. My point here is that as you move on in your life and in your head, you open doors to alternative opportunities that can make a difference to your future income streams.

Perhaps an inheritance will come your way in the future, and whilst it is not something to rely upon, it is a factor to weigh up that could sway your decisions and timelines. Exploring other avenues, through divesting possessions that are not of sentimental value to you but likely to yield a fair price, is also worth including in your income source.

And of course, when seeking to enhance your earnings through these alternative endeavours, it's important to include any taxes that may be due in your pros and cons assessment. You don't want any unexpected surprises to await you down the line due to an undeclared income source.

With some foresight and planning, these opportunities to be more frugal and enterprising can be used to plug gaps which may at first seem too big to tackle. And if luck happens to be on your side too, your glidepath to your life beyond can end up looking all the more attainable. There's a saying that you make your own luck in life, and I believe that this follows from taking decisive actions to behave with a prosperous mindset and grow your potential – which will sometimes take you out of your comfort zone – to attain the lifestyle you not only need but also ultimately desire in your life beyond the 9 to 5.

6

ABOUT YOUR HEALTH AND WELLBEING

I've touched a little bit on the importance of your emotional and physical health as you get ready for your future life beyond, but I feel it warrants a whole focus area on its own – in fact, probably a whole new book. Everything you aim for is centred on you being fit and healthy to enjoy your new freedoms, and I want to dedicate some time for you, particularly as you get older, to learn more about being smart with your actions and impacts and try to make wiser decisions.

In the interests of full transparency, I have no special expertise in this area, just common sense that I sometimes put to the test and at other times completely ignore. Whilst I know what's good for me generally, I am not always the most dedicated with my diet and exercise regimes, often not following any particular plan and just allowing myself freedom, which I inevitably need to reign in at times before things go too awry and I no longer recognise the person reflected in the mirror.

You spent some time at the beginning of your journey contemplating who you are and your personality type. Now I'd like you to take a closer look at yourself in the mirror.

Do you like what you see?

You might prefer to have fewer lines and grey roots appearing and perhaps fewer (or more) pounds around your waistline.

Do you feel fit and healthy?

You might feel that you could be fitter and healthier.

Are you happy?

Is the face you see content and reflective of a life well lived so far and with more to offer?

What changes do you wish to make, if any?

If you notice areas where you could benefit from some care and attention, then my suggestion is to start from the inside and work your way outwards.

MENOPAUSE/ANDROPAUSE

I first want to acknowledge that many of you embarking upon your glidepath might be encountering multiple changes within yourself right now that impact all aspects of how you relate to the world around you. Whilst the impact of diminishing oestrogen levels in women and transgender men can be sudden and severe, men and transgender women do not completely escape, with a gradual decline in testosterone leading to some similar experiences. Common features include:

- Lack of energy

- Mood changes

- Low libido

- Hot sweats

- Poor sleep

- Forgetfulness or "brain fog"

You might be caught off guard and think you are going crazy if you have not already recognised this transition taking place within you. Your own body's natural ageing process may debilitate you and cause you to suffer in multiple ways if you do not know when to seek help.

There are better times ahead if you are currently in the throes of this turmoil. In her brilliant book, *The Menopause Brain*, Dr Lisa Mosconi shares the evidence that after menopause, women's bodies have a reawakening, and in a survey of Danish women, 62% confirmed a stronger sense of wellbeing after menopause than they felt before, and similarly, 65% of British women were happier after menopause than their younger selves.

A book men may find particularly helpful is *Ageing and the Andropause: Reclaim Your Youth with Testosterone Replacement Therapy* by Ross Tomkins, as it explores both physical and emotional changes and provides the practical strategies to approach this phase of your life with grace and resilience to optimise your wellbeing.

These ageing processes, in addition to those you are embarking upon in your working life, can sometimes seem overwhelming, but you do have the necessary tools and resources to help you cope and ultimately thrive.

YOUR MIND

Weighing in at around 3 lbs or 1.36 kg, your brain is around 60% fat, making it the fattiest organ in your body. How ironic that the organ that controls your every thought and motivation about how you are, and that works tirelessly night and day to ensure your body is as synchronised as possible, still retains its high fat content – which you don't ever want to lose, unlike fat that may be deposited around other areas of your body. Your brain remains out of sight and, for the most part, unnoticed, but as you age, you might start to take more interest in what's actually going on in there. As you enter and travel along your glidepath, this interest might become more intense, to the point that you start to question everything about your decisions and possibly over-analyse your motives and goals.

I too, experience moments of doubt when I question whether I have made the right choices and notions of self-sabotage invade my thoughts, when I fear I have taken a wrong turn. In my early career, I read *Feel the Fear and Do It Anyway* by Susan Jeffers, and it gave me a sense of adventure to push on with my ambitions. I recently re-read it, and I was struck by its simplicity and relevance to me today as I enter my late career phase with its striking messaging: "If you knew you could handle anything that came your way, what would you possibly have to fear?"

It felt like a homecoming, reassuring me that I am indeed on the right track with the plans I have designed for myself and that I have the capacity and courage to alter them if necessary. The answer to the question is, of course, "Nothing!"

Having and growing a healthy mindset as a powerful ally for the attainment of your goals is to be prioritised and nurtured. If you've only paid scant regard to your brain up to now, it's time to start heeding signs and making the necessary adjustments to keep your neurons in tip-top condition.

Your Brain-Chemistry

Your brain is balanced with multiple and intricate combinations of neurotransmitters, enzymes and hormones that play a crucial role in how you feel, how you think and how you act. Unlike other cells in your body that grow and renew, your brain neurons are mostly irreplaceable, and how you treat them will make a difference in how you live your life.

Your neurotransmitters do what the name says: they transmit messages from nerve endings to and between your brain cells. Some familiar ones are:

- *Serotonin* – This is your feel-good messenger that brings you sensations of happiness and helps you feel relaxed and confident. When your serotonin levels are low, you are more likely to feel anxious and depressed.

- *Dopamine* – This is your reward messenger that motivates and helps you derive pleasure from your actions.

Perhaps less commonly known are:

- *Norepinephrine* – This keeps you alert, helps you to concentrate and affects your mood.

- *GABA (gamma-aminobutyric acid)* – This is your calm messenger that helps to reduce anxiety.

These connections can alter the circuitry of your brain, and if you are intent on having more positive experiences and forming habits that make you feel good, you can shape your mind to be stronger.

Mindfulness

There is a lot in your favour as you age. One of the benefits is your ability to be more aware of the present moment and be "mindful" to engage with your surroundings and who is in front of you now rather than constantly thinking about other matters that distract you and divide your attention.

You are more predisposed than your younger self to better take to emotional mindfulness as you are generally able to switch off and not react or be judgemental in the moment. Cultivating a mindfulness approach can help you when faced with life's challenges by improving your focus, calmness and relationship with stress. It can also have health benefits, supporting better sleep and reducing pain and depression.

There are many ways to practice mindfulness, and practice is definitely a requirement to hone this skill. This can be through formal meditation and focused breathing, paying attention to your breath and its rhythm; being observant and noticing your thoughts and environment without getting caught up in them;

131

and cultivating feelings of empathy towards yourself and others.

The Mental Health Foundation recommends that acts of kindness be built into business decisions and government policy as there are clear benefits to society, including reducing stress and improving emotional wellbeing, with resulting positive impacts on business outcomes and productivity. To begin your mindfulness journey, you could start with acts of kindness like registering to help a local good cause or checking in on a friend you haven't seen in a while.

There are many examples of people who have completed their glidepath journey becoming ambassadors and fund-raisers for their own organisation's good causes. Others support their local communities by delivering groceries, hot meals and other essential items to housebound neighbours. Simply spending time conversing with them or reading to them when they are incapacitated or losing their sight is highly valued. Schools and hospitals benefit from such kindness in similar ways through planned visits to support children's literacy and patients who have no relations nearby.

When you do others a service in a kind way, this promotes brain activity, releasing the serotonin and dopamine molecules that in turn make you happy. Your self-esteem is improved, which builds your confidence and your strength to withstand the knocks you might take in your everyday life. By acting kindly, you can derive as much, if not more, pleasure and satisfaction as your recipient.

Benefits of Meditation

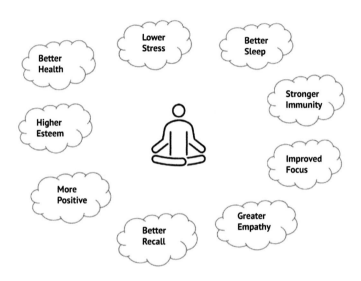

You can appreciate there are multiple benefits to practicing mindful meditation, but it's not enough to just know this. It's a case of getting started and maintaining the momentum to keep going until it becomes a habit. I previously mentioned that establishing habits can take longer than you might imagine, and there are a number of apps widely available, such as *Headspace*, *Calm* and *Ten Percent Happier*, with which you can set daily reminders to put aside quality, mindful time to concentrate, breathe and lose yourself in this space for a few moments.

If you've never practiced mindfulness before, take a few moments now to find a quiet place to sit or lie down.

Exhale all air completely from your mouth.

Inhale deeply through your nose for a count of four seconds.

Hold your breath for a count of seven seconds.

Exhale loudly out of your mouth for a count of eight seconds.

Repeat this process a few times.

Choose an everyday item to observe; it could be a cup, a pen or a leaf from a plant.

Get yourself into a comfortable position.

Concentrate on your selected item.

Observe its colour, its material, its texture and its shape.

Notice anything else that you might have missed – does it make a sound? Is it hard? Is it soft? Does it smell? Does it shine?

Using your breathing technique, stay present with your chosen object for a few minutes.

Congratulations! You have just completed two mindfulness approaches. Your breathing mindfulness is based on an ancient yogic technique called pranayama, developed by Dr Andrew Weil, who refers to it as "the natural tranquiliser of the nervous system". Your observational or visualisation mindfulness has roots in Buddhism. Mindfulness approaches help to "still" the mind by bringing you intimately into the present moment, or they can help activate your responses through the engagement of your senses and your brain neurons. They are mind-strengthening practices that serve to exercise your brain and promote your calm and positive outlook, which help you to cope better with everyday stresses and distractions that can be overwhelming if left unchecked.

With any habit, it's important to find the approaches that best suit you so you will be comfortable repeating them and developing your skills accordingly. Carving out a few minutes each day for a mindful moment is a powerful way to enhance your wellbeing, and you can fit it in during everyday tasks like household chores or, if you prefer, in your exercise routines or more formal daily rituals.

Journalling

You can also improve your mental health by noting down your thoughts and feelings. This provides a way to feel grounded and place in context your emotions. It can help you to unscramble jumbled-up thoughts about your concerns and anxieties and allay your worst fears.

When you write, you are able to externalise key issues that might affect you, and putting words down on paper can often provide the clarity that is elusive when retained in your head. Journalling helps to build resilience by revealing to you better ways to cope when you are able to express your difficulties outwardly. This is achieved through offloading your concerns, isolating them and identifying how you are best able to deal with them. A problem shared is a problem halved as the saying goes, even if it is only to yourself in your private journal.

Other health benefits reported, include a reduction in anxiety and depression, where deeper thoughts and feelings explored through the medium of writing can help manage the extent of these conditions.

Journalling can also act as a memory jogger when you reflect on your progress, supporting you to have better recall and retention.

Dr Judy Willis, neurologist and authority on brain research, extols the cognitive benefits of journalling since "the practice of writing can enhance the brain's intake, processing, retaining and retrieving of information…it promotes the brain's attentive focus…boosts long-term memory, illuminates patterns, gives the brain time for reflection, and when well-guided, is a source of conceptual development and stimulus of the brain's highest cognition".

Some tips to help you get started with your journalling include:

Writing in your preferred style – this could be in a purpose-made journal, in a notebook, on your laptop or even as a recorded voice note.

Writing at your own pace – this could be as little as 5 or 10 minutes a day. It's more important to have a daily or weekly routine than writing copiously but infrequently.

Being free – don't hold anything back. Be open without judgement or censorship. You're not aiming for perfection here.

Being varied – write about everything and anything: your memories, your feelings, your experiences, what you have learned and what you hope to achieve.

Being consistent – allocate a set time every day, every other day or weekly, whichever strikes the right note to ensure you stick to it.

Action: Think about your day and how you can fit in your mindful moments. How long will you allocate? What approach will you choose?

Action: Think about your week and how you can fit in your journalling moments. What medium best suits you?

By starting your mindfulness journey, you have earned your twelfth key.

KEY #12

I will repeat for good measure that habits take time and practice to form, but you know and appreciate their value once you are in an established rhythm, and it's good to keep reminding yourself of the benefits that lie ahead when you are in these early stages of their creation.

Memory

Among the benefits of meditation and journalling is enhancing your attention and concentration levels, which support better memory retention and recall. If, like me, with a family history of Alzheimer's disease and a memory impacted by menopause, you have concerns creeping in about whether you are experiencing the onset of a progressive and degenerative condition or whether this is a temporary status that will eventually resolve itself on its own, taking affirmative action is the best way to address your concerns.

Your brain circuitry or neuroplasticity grows stronger through the neurotransmitter connections you make, and the more you challenge yourself, the more pathways are formed through these new experiences. Pushing yourself outside your comfort zone and taking up learning opportunities, such as a new language or a new skill, or testing your knowledge with quizzes and brain games can all support your brain health.

You could test yourself today by:

• Ditching the calculator and trying to work out the answers to common arithmetical questions whenever you come across them. The next time you shop, add up in your mind what you think the total bill will be when you get to the checkout, even if you do so online.

• Having some fun with friends and taking the blindfold Taste-Bud Test that requires you to engage with more of your senses, which enhances your recall.

• Thinking about your location and drawing a map of your area from memory. You can expand this idea to drawing a map of your town or country.

• Taking up a new sport or hobby. Physical activities that use your fine motor skills, such as playing an instrument, knitting, drawing or exercising, improve your coordination and stimulate connections between your brain and your body.

Another irony is that the more you push these boundaries, the less fear you harbour about your future and your ability to cope. Whilst your brain may account for just 2% of your body weight, it uses 20% of your energy supply, and ensuring a positive source of energy to encourage the healthy growth of your brain connections is even more important now as you might at times start to struggle with your recall and your motivations to try new experiences.

YOUR BODY

Nutrition

"You are what you eat" is often cited to encourage better decisions in relation to food. Understanding what works best for your body and mind as you age is important. You need to know what to feed yourself in essential nutrients that support your thinning bones and skin and provide the energy to your brain and other vital organs to carry on the round-the-clock business of sustaining you.

Hopefully, you have reached your stage of life aware of the sources of food that you ought to avoid, not only because they adversely affect you from your own biological make-up but also from a health perspective.

The late Dr Michael Mosley was a strong advocate of the Mediterranean-style diet, with it being nutrient-rich and high in protein and fibre with fewer carbohydrates to support patients in lowering their blood sugar levels and cholesterol and reversing their diabetic conditions. This is a diet also favoured by many leading health practitioners and heralded as the world's healthiest with protective benefits for your brain, heart, digestive tract and hormones, supporting reduced risks of heart attack, stroke, cancer, obesity, depression and dementia.

So, what is this amazing diet that promises such great health benefits?

The Mediterranean diet is mainly plant-based with small amounts of seafood, eggs or poultry added to provide variety. It has no refined sugars or processed foods, little red meat and is mainly based on fresh fruits and vegetables (ideally the leafy-green variety), whole grains, beans, lentils, nuts and seeds. Plant oils such as extra virgin olive oil with vinegar and lemon are used as dressings, and herbs and spices provide the flavourings. A glass of red wine or an espresso coffee might round off a meal, with both being good sources of antioxidants, which protect against cell damage and slow the ageing process. As the diet is not too restrictive, there is a high chance of sticking with it since occasional treats are permitted, making it a more appealing food regime to follow.

What you won't find in this type of diet are fried or fatty foods; sugary foods, like bread, cakes and biscuits; or fizzy drinks – all of which tend to provide you with an insulin spike followed by a sluggish feeling due to a drop in blood sugar levels. These foods generally contain a high number of calories and lead to craving more foods with no nourishing qualities.

To educate you further on the benefits of "eating a rainbow" when you approach your food choices, you could select these options in your healthier diet plan:

- *Flavonoids* and *Flavonols* are beneficial to your heart, helping to reduce blood pressure and cholesterol. Examples are cocoa, apples, berries, citrus fruits and tea.

- *Carotenoids* help prevent cancer and also support optical health. Examples are carrots, peppers, tomatoes and pumpkins.

- *Polyphenols* support brain health and longevity. Examples are dark chocolate, berries, pears, grapes and red wine.

- *Phytosterols* help regulate cholesterol and are another source of nutrients to support your heart. Examples are nuts, seeds and legumes (beans, peas and lentils).

- *Phytoestrogens* are especially important for women to support oestrogen levels if taken consistently. Examples include soybeans, lentils, chickpeas, apricots, dates, flaxseeds, sesame seeds, wheat, rye, pistachios and almonds.

• *Glucosinolates* are detoxifiers, which are good for digestion and lowering cancer risk, especially colon cancer. Examples include cruciferous vegetables like broccoli, cauliflower, kale and Brussels sprouts.

A good friend turned her diabetes diagnosis around by adopting the Mediterranean approach, and her salads were the most colourful and flavoursome I have ever encountered, containing at least 10 but often 15 or more different ingredients. It's enough to make you want to reject the sad options at your supermarket and be far more adventurous with your colours and choices, and not be deceived either by some of the so-called healthy options that are, in fact, just disguised processed foods.

Many of these good foods, such as kale, spinach, red cabbage, artichokes, pecans, beets and berries, also contain high levels of antioxidants. If you need a sweet treat, dark chocolate is also in this food group. Another close friend who spent some time as a food taster was always appreciative when the high cocoa content chocolate arrived for taste tests rather than the high milk and fat variety as the latter was so cloying on her palate, which had become more attuned to better quality ingredients.

Add to the mix cranberries, cherries, fish (such as salmon and pilchards), dairy products (like Greek yoghurt), plant-based drinks and fortified orange juice to support your ageing bones and joints, and you have a whole store of goodness to choose from.

You get the idea. Following a diet for its nutritional content rather than its impact on your waistline has got to be the best way forward. Being more selective in your food choices and steering clear of, or at least avoiding where you can, heavily processed foods, containing high levels of trans fats and sugar, will support your ageing process and enhance your cognition whilst providing energy to your vital organs to carry on doing what they do best – protecting and sustaining you into the future.

Exercising

Now, let's be clear on one thing: I am not going to preach to anyone about their exercise regimes as I would be in the "Do as I say, not as I do" category, and I tend to fall in and out of good exercise habits, just as I do my eating ones. Being conscious too, that we are all different shapes and sizes and all at varying levels of fitness, it would be foolhardy to even try to prescribe what is best for you. What I do wish to advise is how you might be smarter about your choices to yield the best returns as your body and mind age.

I like simplicity and fact-based evidence of what actually works, so I suggest concentrating your efforts where the science supports the actions. British statesman Edward Stanley (1826-1893) once said, "*Those who think they have no time for bodily exercise will sooner or later have to find time for illness.*" This quote motivates me to practice some form of exercise in my daily life, even if it's a 5- or 10-minute "mindfulness with movement" break.

And if it's been a while, you can start with basic movements. The one-legged balance test is a strong indicator of your health in later life. Research predicts that if you are able to balance on one leg for at least 10 seconds, you are more likely to live longer, as good balance reflects muscle strength, a stable core and good coordination, meaning you are at a lower risk of falls.

When you exercise, a number of changes take place in your body. Endorphins, known as your body's natural painkillers, are released in the brain, which can support pain management by blocking pain signals and effectively switching your pain receptors off. This natural pain relief can help you function and control the level of discomfort you have. Serotonin and dopamine, your happy and reward transmitters, lift your spirits, and you can better manage your stress hormone, cortisol, to enhance your overall sense of wellbeing. A few good enough reasons already to exercise. And if you happen to be experiencing menopause, studies show that moderate exercise reduces hot sweats and improves the quality of your sleep. Another two great reasons. In a study of older people who regularly exercised, 35% had a lower risk of developing dementia than those who didn't. And there are more great reasons in abundance if you just think about it, not least making you more agile and able to cope better and go about your day-to-day business with a spring in your step rather than feeling tired and sluggish.

If you have an office-based job or work from home in virtual and hybrid environments, possibly on make-do or make-shift furniture that was never ergonomically designed or intended to be used as a permanent office space, then your body will bear the sins of poor posture and behaviour – eventually. Simple daily stretches can help iron out the creases and loosen your limbs after extended periods of time hunched over your gadgets. I wonder how telling this will be on our younger generations in due course, with their heads always arched downwards to their mobile devices.

As you age, exercising in a moderately intense way is considered optimal, and whilst for men, there are some benefits to undertaking high-intensity training, the opposite is true for women.

Exercise Intensity

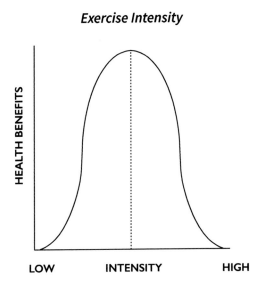

Discovering what best suits your lifestyle and tastes will benefit you long-term and ensure you commit to daily routines. Some of you will need the discipline of a gym class, whilst a brisk 30-minute walk, three times a week, will work fine for others. For your wellbeing, you might want to choose Tai Chi, strengthening with weights and bands for bone density and Yoga or Pilates for flexibility.

You don't necessarily need to spend any money to get fitter, you just need to make more of an effort to move your body, which you can do without any fancy equipment or wardrobe. Strength training, such as squats, press-ups and lunges, yields particularly positive results in developing muscle mass and cognitive performance and can be done anywhere and anytime. The point is to move your body repetitively and consistently to establish good habits.

BREAKING HABITS

You've concentrated mainly on forming good habits in this chapter, but how do you approach the undoing of practices you have established, as you make your preparations for your life beyond? Habits are as varied and diverse as you are human, ranging from your spending, sleeping, eating and drinking (and other substances you might consume) to your social interactions and work practices.

I am just as guilty as the next person with bad habits formed in my life, such as the long hours propped at my dining room table with my laptop, hunched over my keyboard. I have no excuses, as I have all the resources and materials I need to work with a good posture, and I am aware of the rights and wrongs of workstation design and comfort. Yet, I continue to work in my habitual way that I know isn't right for me.

To try to understand your behaviour and turn the negative practices you'd like to change into positive ones, you can break down your habits into three manageable steps, that together form the habit loop:

1. Cue – the "what" that attracts you

2. Behaviour – the "how" you react

3. Reward – the "why" you do what you do on repeat

Take a simple example, like being on a diet and desiring chocolate. The cue is the chocolate, and you can behave by either giving in to your desire or not. The reward is tasting the chocolate, which you will repeat over and over for as long as you desire it. In fact, the more you repeat the process, the more automated your brain becomes, until you are not even consciously aware of making informed choices. Driving home from work is a clear example where the familiarity of the route is so carved out in your brain's neural pathways that often you arrive home without remembering your journey, conserving your brain energy in doing so.

Breaking established habits takes conscious effort, and this takes more energy as you are making new and different connections in your brain. Being on a diet and resisting the chocolate takes effort as you need to distract yourself from the alluring thing you most desire in the moment. In the same way, breaking the routine of your working week requires forethought and adherence to a new approach or you can slip back into your habitual ways.

To help you change your poor habits, think about a good habit you currently practice. Break it down into the steps above. What makes your good habit something you want to do repeatedly? Can you apply this to the habit you wish to change for the better? For me, it was to change my habit of working at my dining room table when I had a perfectly good office already set up in my outside garden room. To change my approach, I simply needed to increase the allure of going outside, which the addition of a kettle and a mini fridge did for me, as I no longer had to dodge the raindrops of our typical English weather whenever I wanted a brew.

Action: Think about the habits you'd like to change. What will you do differently when faced with the same cue next time? Or what about a new habit you wish to establish? What are the cues you need to encourage your repeat behaviour?

In recognition of your growing courage to tackle tough challenges, here's your thirteenth key. Just one more key to go!

KEY #13

Knowing the cues that trigger your response is the first step to forming your new commitment. This could be a certain place or time, a sequence of events or even an individual that evokes the behaviour you wish to change. Identifying a new reward for your changed behaviour to entice you to stick to your new path will also help you. And you don't need to make big strides overnight – slow and steady wins the race. This could mean, for example, shrinking your workday by an hour and gradually to two hours and more, as opposed to taking full days off in the early stages of your glidepath. A change of environment may also help. By replacing my habit of sitting at my dining room table with going to my outside garden room, my posture is better supported and I also have fewer distractions, which improves my focus and my ability to concentrate.

One of the best forms of support is from your friends and family, who can offer you the encouragement you need to carry on, and it compels you to take responsibility to achieve your goals if you share your intentions with them. When I first thought about writing this book, I said it out loud to a couple of my close friends and family members who immediately got behind me, offering me ideas and people I could speak to in their networks. It made me more inclined to go through with it and, in fact, motivated me to see this project through to its completion.

Being patient with yourself if you lapse and forgiving yourself for any transgression is part of your growth in moving away from a position of weakness towards a position of strength. Using visualisation to imagine yourself arriving and remaining in your position of strength will boost your confidence and motivate you to achieve the success you desire.

Manifesting good outcomes and expressing gratitude for the progress you make, no matter how small, keeps you mindfully present, preventing relapse into the automaton state your brain takes on with your old habits. How many of you have driven to your old home after moving to a new address, where you just so easily slip back into autopilot mode when you get into your car? I have other examples where I have tried to change things but not quite got to the 'established' stage for my new habit and have retreated back to where I was before, whether with exercise and dietary changes or just committing to doing something differently, like using OneNote instead of Word to organise my documents. I'd love to say I've mastered that last one but I am still drawn back to my old ways for now.

You've likely made resolutions at New Year at one time or another, but how many of them did you actually follow through with? It's really important to celebrate your progress after each and every milestone, no matter how small the step is in the overall plan of your life beyond, so that you reinforce your changed behaviour positively and increase your chances of success.

YOUR APPEARANCE

Your health and wellbeing actually begin on the inside, with how you nurture and care for yourself. This shows up in your body – your skin, your face and your demeanour. When you feel great, you wear this feeling externally. As world-class French designer Coco Chanel observed, "*Nature gives you the face you have at twenty; it is up to you to merit the face you have at fifty.*"

How many of you look great wearing a scowl or a frown? Not only does it make you appear unapproachable and unwelcoming, it ages you, creating deep furrows on your forehead and around your eyes and mouth. With less energy required, smiling enhances your wellbeing and appearance – and it's also infectious.

The simple act of smiling actually bolsters your mood by releasing those endorphins that produce your feel-good hormones and lowering your stress hormones. This results in better concentration and feeling less anxious. It also contributes to higher self-esteem and emotional resilience, making you better able to bounce back from any setbacks.

The next time you are out and about, wear a smile when coming across the path of others and see how many smile back. You'll likely be pleasantly surprised.

As you progress on your glidepath, this doesn't mean that you let your standards of self-care drop and remain in bed on days you would otherwise be en-route to the office or in your home office. It affords you the time to invest in yourself and enhance nature's gifts. If you start your day ready to face the world rather than remaining in your bedclothes or track pants, this already gives you a sense of purpose to accomplish the goals you have set for yourself. I am in regular contact with an old neighbour who, even though she has lived alone for many years and is now in her mid-eighties, always puts on her makeup, whether she has guests or not, and always has a ready smile and a real joie de vivre despite any aches and pains her ageing body might present on the day.

When you put your best foot forward, whether or not you leave your home to face the day, you set yourself up for a positive outlook that reflects well on you and your future prospects. This is a time to invest in yourself, to respect yourself for what you have accomplished and to enjoy the rewards of your toils.

7

YOUR LIFE BEYOND THE 9 TO 5

I am writing this chapter with a little way still to go on my own glidepath, and as I pre-empt my new reality, I am filling in the blanks with conversations and experiences shared by others who have already arrived in this place.

What has stood out for me in my interviews with people who have already reached their life beyond, is that they had no regrets about their decisions to leave work in their rear-view mirror and were looking forward to their new beginnings. In fact, many admitted they did not know where they had previously found the time to hold down a full-time position as their lives were filled with social activities in their communities and pursuing interests of their own choosing.

One respondent said that what they feared most was not knowing the kind of things they would need to worry about, but the reality was so very different. They had a relaxed and enjoyable outlook and used their time to fulfil their own agenda rather than that of others. This person had held down a high-pressured role in marketing and had begun to resent the demands they faced with endless requests and no satisfaction derived from their completion as more would just arrive to fill the void. Whilst stopping work was not necessarily on their immediate horizon, a change of circumstances brought their decision forward, and without the luxury of much planning or forethought, they were able to replace their stressful life with a more fulfilled one that just didn't entail going into the office or online each day.

The rest of you, having more planning time on your side, can also look forward to this day, with less worry and fear, for which you can give yourself some credit for having the benefit of foresight.

WHAT WILL YOUR FIRST DAY AND WEEK LOOK LIKE?

My first recommendation is to heed some advice from Dr Rangan Chatterjee, who extols the virtues of getting outside in the morning. In his book, *The 4 Pillar Plan*, Dr Chatterjee explains the benefits of morning light through your pupils and onto your skin to support your mental wellbeing. The maximum light strength that you are ever going to get indoors in a bright room, is 500 lux, whereas even on a cloudy day you will receive 10,000 lux, rising to 30,000 lux when the sun is out. The best light is in the morning, and it can help your body's rhythms as you adjust to your new regime. Having your morning brew outdoors, no matter the weather, will be the best start you can give yourself before you even decide what to wear for the day ahead.

Even better would be to combine this with an early morning walk and begin to reach your 10,000 daily steps, or whatever you can comfortably achieve. The benefits of a morning walk are multiple with a boost hit of Vitamin D, which is essential for your bone health and immune system, helping you to fight off colds, flu and other illnesses. Being outdoors helps regulate your circadian rhythm, which supports better sleep patterns and your overall wellbeing. Exercising outside also supports serotonin production, which you know helps alleviate anxiety and depression with its feel-good effects. If you suffer from seasonal affective disorder or SAD syndrome, then a morning walk can be highly beneficial.

When I visualise my first day, after my morning walk or whatever exercise I favour on that particular day, I anticipate filling it with social activities, either meeting up with friends or spending time supporting my chosen charities or, ideally, both. Carving out time for my new hobbies and the community groups with which I have registered might also be appropriate on my first day, or I might sprinkle some of these brighter moments across my week to have a purpose to get up and be out and about.

Your first day and your first week are momentous, and how you start will set the tone for the rest of your days at leisure. Remaining at home, lounging in your pyjamas or spending all your time on cleaning and toil are to be avoided. You want to strike the right balance and start off with clearly defined good habits to establish within the daily and weekly framework that you are beginning to construct.

What Kinds of Activities Will You Undertake?

Being mindful of your reduced income, you'll want to be practical in your commitments and the work and activities you undertake for yourself and others. You looked at some of these activities in your earlier preparatory stages, with some of the more green-fingered among you for instance, choosing to spend a few hours lending nature a hand, perhaps even growing your own organic, nutrient-rich vegetables to support your better diet now that you recognise their cognitive and health attributes.

You might use the talents you employed during your working life to provide support to those in your community who could benefit from your insights and advice. You could find an outlet in mentoring and coaching or even establishing a side-line to generate some income from the activities you pursue now through your own passions and interests rather than necessity. These could be creative activities like cooking, baking, painting, crafting, woodwork or jewellery-making. I had a particularly talented and inspiring friend, sadly no longer with us, who created her own range of cards for every occasion, and she enjoyed not only the process of their production but also the opportunities to meet new people at craft fairs and events, benefitting her social network and her pocket.

Men may benefit in joining organisations such as "Men's Sheds" that promote social connections through coming together as a useful neighbourhood resource to mend or make products and to support local community projects. A friend has had impressive features added to her garden from the endeavours of members of her local branch, including an inscribed bench to commemorate an anniversary.

You might choose to help with outdoor events such as galas and fetes or even major entertaining and sporting events. Rotary International is an organisation that welcomes public support for community projects and there are many other worthy causes that would benefit from your skills and time.

There is no shortage of activities, from volunteering and fundraising to more entrepreneurial and consulting experiences, where you may continue to have social engagement, whether paid or not, that provides you with the fulfilment you deserve to have in your life beyond.

What Best Suits You?

You have taken a peek into yourself and you know what makes you tick and the kind of social and cultural activities you think are best to promote your wellbeing and fill your time. You might prefer solitary activities and find your peace and excitement in fishing, swimming or collecting objects or memorabilia, or you might be more at home with team-based sports and social gatherings.

You should ensure that you don't discount opportunities that come your way and instantly dismiss them because of your inclinations up to this point in your life. There might be associations that you don't find immediately appealing, but you have the time to explore everything on your doorstep, and you may be pleasantly surprised by simply giving them a go. It could be that you've never trodden the boards at your local amateur dramatics group or sung in a choir, both of which have become so popular in recent times for supporting health and wellbeing – and you don't even need to be able to sing all that well. Keeping your options open and treating your time as a means to explore new things will stimulate your mind and benefit you physically as you move with purpose towards your next adventure.

Many established actors held previous careers before hitting the big time. Danny DeVito was once a hairdresser and Harrison Ford a carpenter. Buster Merryfield, who starred in the BBC comedy series *Only Fools and Horses*, had a near 40-year career in banking before becoming a professional actor at the age of 57. Swapping out your career for your passions can lead to unexpected opportunities. One example is a colleague who found herself working in her local tourist office and giving talks about historical events and characters, being very happy to be immersed in this new scene.

Taking Your First Steps

It can be a little daunting initially, showing up at a venue where you don't know a soul. You don't want to miss out on a whole new life chapter if you are inclined to be socially awkward when first meeting others or if you have deep-seated anxieties about taking this initial step. You can take comfort in knowing that you're not alone and can employ a few of the strategies that you have under your belt now, including your breathing and visualisation techniques, to manifest positive outcomes and feel at ease.

If you struggle, you could also take positive action by seeking a mentor, perhaps someone who has already begun their life beyond and is an active participant in local activities. Reminding yourself of your value and the positive contributions that you can now make will improve your confidence and esteem, especially when you are physically able to lend a hand to support others who are not. Distracting yourself from your own concerns by helping others has a way of diminishing them by not giving them the strength or importance to warrant your attention.

You might own a car and be able to offer a lift to someone in need or walk an elderly or infirm person's dog where they are no longer capable of doing so themselves. This is one activity that a colleague who recently finished work is looking forward to taking up. Having lost her own pet, she signed up with a charity and was put in touch with a gentleman who is now housebound and cannot exercise his dog. This kindness is mutually beneficial as it provides for her the purpose to get up and go outside in the fresh air, the exercise she needs and wants, the social interaction she desires with other dog walkers and the connection she misses having with a pet– and it costs her nothing but time, which she now has in abundant supply.

All changes take some adjustment, and this probably counts as one of the biggest moves you'll make since you launched your career, so if everything hasn't already quite fallen into place as you wanted or expected, then it may just be a matter of time and perseverance and learning to adapt. Building your resilience to bounce back from any setbacks and learning to cope with unexpected outcomes or delayed progress in certain areas are all part of your life beyond. How you handle yourself and your circumstances play into your confidence and how you come to belong in your new world.

A different scenario that you may encounter is not being able to break the bonds that tie you to your past work and finding yourself continuously asked to return for briefing sessions or to support your new replacement. Whilst you may wish to retain some ties as part of your alumni network, how do you politely say, "No, thank you" and not cause offence? I am conscious of this scenario as I have first-hand experience with a member of my own team whose expertise was highly regarded, and who was asked to carry on working when she wanted to move forward with her new life beyond. She was incredibly understanding and reached a happy compromise for a period of time, on her own terms, which suited everyone until we all managed to adjust and get on without her daily presence.

You too, can reach a mutually acceptable outcome by cushioning any requests with kindness, expressing appreciation for the offer and making clear that you are not able to assist on this occasion. Ordinarily, it might be that you would love to help, but your circumstances make it impossible this time. If feasible, offer an alternative solution or suggest another person you rate highly. Over time, the dependency will wane if you are not always so readily available on demand. In my network, a person who was new to serving as a magistrate in the criminal courts was always the one the police would approach to sign off on a search or arrest warrant, no matter the time of day or night. Often, she would be woken up in the small hours until she made the decision to not be available on each and every occasion they came calling, and the police soon adapted to contacting others in an emergency.

You might also wish to extricate yourself from certain commitments you agreed to in the initial stages of your life beyond, as you begin exploring new ventures and activities. Using a polite but assertive approach will assure you of an exit whilst leaving the door open if you wish to resume contact again.

YOUR PARTNER

It's not just your own life that is taking on a whole new look and meaning; for many of you in relationships, this can be a big upheaval in your partner's lifestyle too. Some partners may see this as their opportunity to start organising your calendar and prescribing the best way for you to spend your time and with whom they choose for you rather than giving you the well-earned freedom to choose for yourself. Others might resent sharing so much of their space with you as you now spend more time at home when before you may have been at the office all day.

It's perhaps not a coincidence that there is a demographic trend of an increasing divorce rate for so-called "silver-splitters", with 10% of divorcees now being above the age of 65, according to the US Bar Association. Could this be due to couples finding it difficult to adjust when they are omnipresent in each other's lives?

This is one reason why you need to ensure you share and discuss your plans for your life beyond right from the start, involving your partner in all your preparations and every stage of your transition. Communication is absolutely essential so that you arrive at this place with at least some clarity about what your days of leisure might look like, what activities you might wish to undertake, who you might want to share your space and time with and how your partner might fit into the overall framework of your new life. You don't want your partner to be caught off guard and feel left out or try to take over and unduly influence the picture of the future you have envisioned for yourself. Ideally, you will already have reached a mutual understanding and acceptance of how things will be and will be ready to embrace a different way of life, together.

If that's not the case, catching any potential cause for future conflict early on is paramount to your success and happiness in your new way of life. You've seen how burying your head like an ostrich doesn't support your financial growth, and it won't help you achieve your desired lifestyle now either. You must be clear and assertive in your relationship, help your partner to visualise your life beyond just as you have done and work through any differences. For many of you, this will mean strongly protecting your individual identity and continuing to carry on with activities separate from your "couple" status, and for others, it might mean sharing more of the activities you have previously undertaken separately or embarking on new shared projects together. This could be learning something together, like a language, especially if you are keen on certain travel destinations where you can test your knowledge in real settings. Or you may enjoy dancing lessons or attending cookery classes to refine your kitchen skills and palates. Even studying a subject and gaining a formal qualification might appeal to some couples. Whatever the subject matter or activity, there's bound to be something you can do together that will provide the attraction and enjoyment that your life at work has prevented you from pursuing up to now.

Action: Take a moment to identify the activities you are happy to share with your partner and those that must remain individual to you.

In traditional gender roles, behaviours for men and women have often been preordained by society, with historical reliance on the males as the hunter-gatherers and the women as the homemakers. This juxtaposition can become blurred in your life beyond, and you may struggle to understand how your past roles now fit into or relate to the current and future positioning within your relationship. For many men, this can be an especially difficult transition, and it can feel confusing at times with the normal work week being replaced by activities that are designed not to further careers or family prospects but to enhance the quality and enjoyment of their everyday life.

In your life beyond, you will likely encounter some adjustment to any power imbalance that may have pre-existed and might not even have been of any concern up to now. Ensuring an equal share of time and space to explore your independent interests, in addition to your shared ones, will enable you to be authentic and genuine with yourself and each other.

So, how well do you regard your listening skills? This short quiz will enlighten you.

Rate yourself in the following situations and total the score.

0 = Never, 1 = Rarely, 2 = Occasionally, 3 = Often, 4 = Normally

On a scale of 0-100 (100 = highest), what is your strength as a listener? _____

	Question	Score Here
1.	I attempt to listen carefully even if the subject matter bores me	
2.	I accept other people's different viewpoints	
3.	I try to not get defensive when someone expresses strong negative emotions	
4.	I try to identify the emotion behind the person's words	
5.	I prepare for how people will react when I speak	
6.	I record what is necessary to help me remember what I hear	
7.	I listen freely without judging or criticising	
8.	I make eye contact with the person who is speaking to me	
9.	I remain interested even when I am hearing things I don't wish to hear or agree with	
10.	I prevent any distractions that might affect my listening	
11.	I don't ignore difficult questions	
12.	I don't allow a person's physical appearance or expressions to affect my attention	
13.	I avoid reaching premature conclusions	

14.	I learn something, however small, from each person I meet	
15.	I avoid forming my next response while I am listening	
16.	I listen out for main ideas and themes, not just the specific details	
17.	I know what triggers me to react	
18.	I try to think clearly about what I'm trying to convey when I am speaking	
19.	I try to choose the most appropriate time for my communication	
20.	I don't make assumptions that my listeners have a prior level of understanding	
21.	I am normally successful in conveying my information	
22.	I usually select the most appropriate communication type (written, verbal, in-person etc)	
23.	I choose to listen out for more information to what I want to hear	
24.	I allow the speaker to finish without any interruptions	
25.	I am easily able to summarise in my own words what I hear	
	TOTAL	

How did you do?

75-100 = You're likely to be an excellent listener and communicator.

50-74 = You're trying to be a good listener in the main, but there's room for improvement.

25-49 = Some extra practice will help you become a better listener in future.

0-24 = Start to practice your listening skills now.

Encourage your partner to also take this quiz so they may gain some insight into how they can improve themselves and support you better. Learning to actively listen to each other's viewpoints and respect each other's differences and preferences will generate even stronger and more enjoyable shared times ahead.

Your life beyond the 9 to 5 is a time for personal growth, relaxation and the pursuit of your happiness. You have the freedom to choose activities that bring you joy and fulfilment, from resurrecting old hobbies to exploring new experiences. Endless possibilities await; you just need to seek them out and give them a go. If at first you don't particularly enjoy your chosen experiences, familiarity may enhance their appeal. If it doesn't, you have the time to explore alternative options until you settle into your new routines with your partner in tandem, as appropriate.

Now that you've completed this closing stage of your glidepath, with a strong focus on your life beyond the 9 to 5, you can take a bow, give yourself a well-earned pat on the back and collect your final key.

KEY #14

8
SUMMARY

In this book, we have been on a journey together, starting with your initial thoughts about transitioning onto your retirement glidepath. You have considered many aspects that impact upon your state of readiness to commence your life beyond, including the gradual reduction in your working time. And you are taking steps to make this your new reality until your final day of work, when all of your time becomes your own.

You have taken a deep look at yourself, your career, your finances, your health and your aspirations, and you have worked through multiple exercises to identify ways of attaining your goals when you physically depart from your place of employment. Leaving behind your work mentally poses greater challenges, and you have explored how you may develop positive habits to replace your lifetime routines and commitments.

Working out who you are and what motivates you was your first step to understanding how you might navigate your glidepath journey and how you might approach others for help and support to keep you on track. Your employer is a rich source of support to harness and tap into that can enhance your exit strategy. By demonstrating the benefits, such as doubling the ROI from good mentorship programmes, you can promote win-win outcomes for you and your successors. And you know that these need not be complex or expensive initiatives, as many can operate on the goodwill of staff who are already on their glidepath or have started their life beyond.

You have seen that simple acts of kindness can yield positive benefits for the individual and the organisation with elevated esteem and productivity resulting from such considerate behaviours. Focusing on wellbeing and inclusivity to ensure all people, no matter their age, have equal opportunities for growth and development enriches the reputations of organisations as desirable places to work, and it also ensures legal compliance with employment regulations and requirements.

Your financial health greatly impacts your overall health and wellbeing, which is why we took some time to really dissect your finances and spending patterns and identify opportunities to improve your growth potential. You spent time educating yourself on your retirement savings rules and procedures and your tax and social security system to better understand your disposable income and how you may best position yourself to maximise your retirement savings. You closed as many gaps as you could by setting smart goals and being frugal, where appropriate, to support your wealth creation.

Having quality time to care for yourself is a sound investment, not just for your own peace of mind, but is positive societally with fewer dependencies on state-funded institutions, such as in the provision of medical care and means-tested retirement plans. Developing a growth mindset to continually improve yourself, your mind, your body and your outlook is worth the effort, and if you are not immediately successful in your endeavours, you can remember that this is a journey and that you will face challenges, and overall you are heading in the direction that gives you strength and power.

Through the connections and associations you make with others in this part of your life, you are shaping a future that is meaningful to you, productive and ultimately rewarding. You are ready to embrace whatever comes next with confidence and the self-assurance that you will handle yourself, your situation and your circumstances to your advantage.

You have acquired a total of 14 keys along the way, which is not without significance. For anyone who is a fan of numerology, it is a combination of numbers one and four, which add to five and together symbolise new beginnings with firm foundations from where you can embrace change. From a spiritual perspective, it represents transformation and an upward trajectory towards a higher consciousness. From a Biblical sense, it symbolises completion, wholeness and freedom. The number 14 is also associated with independence and creativity.

As you push ahead onto your life beyond the 9 to 5 – numbers that together also make 14 – I wish you good luck with the adventures that await you to be discovered and enjoyed.

WHERE TO FIND MORE INFORMATION

In producing this book, I have shared insights that I have gleaned from other professional authors; from multiple website sources through online searches; and from family, friends, friends of friends, colleagues, colleagues' family members and associates. All were incredibly supportive, offering suggestions and recommendations, and I thank each and every one, for being so forthcoming and enthusiastic with your input.

Where I have cited particularly useful sources, I have included them in the text or added them to the notes section for your reference.

I recommend you take some time to research the plethora of help and advice that is available to you online, in your local library or via recommendations from your network. Whether this is to help you with your finances, your health and wellbeing or your learning and development, there is support and advice readily available to you. And the value of a personal recommendation or self-discovery of support on your doorstep is so much higher than anything I could wish to provide for you here.

ACKNOWLEDGEMENTS

I wish to extend my thanks to the many contributors who gave me their precious time to explore with them the idea of their life beyond and how this could be a more engaging period of their life. I reserve special gratitude for Tracy and Wendy for their unstinting support, creativity and many connections; to the three Marks – Mark 1, Mark 2 (you know who you are) and Mark Shortall – as well as Michael and Thane for their inspiring male insights; to Louis and Xander for their technical expertise; and to Maureen Brett for her honest critique and considerate input – and for always being around when needed.

My colleagues have been so thoughtful and engaged in this subject, and I am grateful for their interest and their willingness to devote the time needed to complete my questionnaire when I know many of them already experience survey fatigue. I am so appreciative of the time given to me by Claudia and the Lowe clan and the joie de vivre so evident in their family. Thanks also to Christian Dahl who continues to be a mentor, advisor and an ardent fan of career modelling for older workers.

I must thank my family for their tolerance and understanding, particularly Ciara, Grace and Luna.

I would not have even contemplated writing a book of this nature were it not for the motivation and encouragement of my coach, Daniel Barnett from the HR Inner Circle, to whom I am most indebted for setting me off on this particular path and keeping me on track to the finish line.

Getting to the finish line has brought me into the world of professionals like Aaron Gaff, to whom I am grateful for sharing thoughts and detailed editing suggestions that helped to shape the final result. My thanks also go to Joshua Goode for his beta read and initial edits and to Tincuta Collet for her artistic designs.

In writing this book, the most joyous aspect has been the people I have been able to interact with, and I thank each and every one of them for being so forthcoming with ideas, for being interested enough to participate in this work, and most of all, for getting ready for the next chapter in their lives beyond the 9 to 5.

NOTES

Chapter 1: Let the Journey Begin

some psychologists hold that humans have a fundamental discomfort e.g. Leon Festinger, *A Theory of Cognitive Dissonance* (1957); Kurt Lewin, *Field Theory in Social Science* (1951).

the human body itself can affect our readiness to embrace change Dr Bruce Lipton, *The Biology of Belief: Unleashing the Power of Consciousness, Matter & Miracles* (2005).

almost half of US households, *The 2022 Survey of Consumer Finances* (2022), *USA Facts Team*, https://usafacts.org/data-projects/retirement-savings.

over seven million people in the UK above the age of 50, *Life Well Spent Report 2023* (2023), *Sun Life*, https://www.sunlife.co.uk/life-well-spent/.

Men born in the United States in 2023 are expected to live, on average, to age 76.9, https://ourworldindata.org/why-do-women-live-longer-than-men.

In India life expectancy for men is lower, at 65.8 years, Aaron O'Neil (2024), Statista.

one in five men are deceased before the age of 65, various sources, including http://www.menshealthforum.org.uk/.

Chapter 2: Who Are You?

Silent Generation from *Younger Generation* (1951), Time Magazine.

DiSC, personality profile based on William Moulton Marston's original behaviour model in his book *Emotions of Normal People* (1928) and subsequent book *DISC, Integrative Psychology* (1931).

Carl Jung, Swiss Psychoanalyst (1875-1961), was also a psychiatrist, psychotherapist and psychologist, as well as a prolific author, whose works include, *The Psychology of the Unconscious* (1912), *The Archetypes and the Collective Unconscious* (1934), and *Man and His Symbols* (1964).

Chapter 3: Where Are You?

the mother has made the most sacrifices in career choices, various sources, including an article by Taylor Borden (2024), LinkedIn News, https://www.linkedin.com/posts/linkedin-news_women-are-more-likely-to-take-career-breaks-activity-7169006706994192387-LtPh.

Maslow's Hierarchy of needs, Abraham Maslow (1908-1970), American psychologist and philosopher.

SMART criteria, credited to George Doran (1981) in *Management Review*.

Loneliness is a common experience among older adults, Lauren Newmyer and Ashton Verdery *Older adult loneliness on the rise around the world* (2023), https://www.niussp.org/individual-and-population-ageing/older-adult-loneliness-on-the-rise-around-the-world/.

It's an apparent myth that a new habit takes approximately three weeks to establish, Signe Dean (2019), https://www.sciencealert.com/here-s-how-long-it-actually-takes-to-break-a-habit-according-to-science.

when she became entitled to receive her government regulated payment, she only received the French part, https://europa.eu/youreurope/citizens/work/retire-abroad/state-pensions-abroad/index_en.htm.

About Schmidt, New Line Cinema (2002), features Jack Nicholson as a retired insurance actuary who tries to continue to offer his services but is declined, and on leaving the building, he sees his life's work put out for waste disposal.

Chapter 4: How Can Organisations Help?

median profits of Fortune 500 countries with mentoring programmes in the US more than double than those of companies without, Sam Cooke, *Mentoring Impact Report* (2024), MentorCliq, https://www.mentorcliq.com/blog/mentoring-impact-report.

Iceland, New Zealand and Japan also host more employees above the age of 55, PricewaterhouseCoopers *Golden Age Index, 2023 Report*, https://www.pwc.co.uk/services/economics/insights/golden-age-index.

The proportion of the world population aged 60 years or more has more than tripled since 1950, United Nations, Department of Economic and Social Affairs Population Division, *World Population Ageing 1950-2050* (2021),https://www.un.org/development/desa/pd/sites/www.un.org.development.desa.pd/files/files/documents/2021/Nov/undesa_pd_2002_wpa_1950-2050_web.pdf.

There are financial benefits, and potential health benefits too, for older workers, Richard Fry and Dana Braga, *Older Workers are Growing in Number and Earning Higher Wages* (2023), https://www.pewresearch.org/social-trends/2023/12/14/older-workers-are-growing-in-number-and-earning-higher-wages/.

three-fifths of its member countries were set to increase their normal retirement ages, OECD *Pensions at a Glance 2023:OECD and G20 Indicators* (2023), OECD Publishing, Paris, https://doi.org/10.1787/678055dd-en.

Chapter 5: About Your Finances

17% of women and 26% of men feel like they are on track to meet their financial goals, https://www.newyorklife.com/newsroom/2023/wealth-watch-2023-hope-despite-inflation-recession.

women having an average fund size of 30% smaller than their male counterparts, World Economic Forum, *3 reasons the retirement crisis is a woman's crisis – and 3 reasons it isn't* (2023), https://www.weforum.org/agenda/2023/08/3-reasons-the-retirement-crisis-is-a-women-s-crisis-and-3-reasons-it-isnt/.

although this might be falling out of favour as being too low to meet current living standards, Lori Konish, *Is it time to rethink the 4% retirement withdrawal rule?* (2024), https://www.cnbc.com/2024/05/13/why-it-might-be-time-to-rethink-the-4percent-retirement-withdrawal-rule.html.

in Singapore, an individual would need around $2.3k per month, Timothy Ho, *How much do I need to save and invest at age 55?* (2024), https://dollarsandsense.sg/retirement-planning-in-singapore-how-much-do-i-need-to-save-and-invest-to-retire-at-age-55/.

US household expenses chart, Connor Brooke, *Consumer Shopping trends and Statistics by the Generation* (2023), https://www.business2community.com/consumer-shopping-trends-and-statistics-by-the-generation-gen-z-millennials-gen-x-boomers-and-the-silents.

the average pot for US family members in 2024 being $87k, Tessa Campbell and Paul Kim, *Average 401(k) Balance by Age in 2024: Benchmarking Your Retirement Savings* (2024), https://www.businessinsider.com/personal-finance/investing/average-401k-balance.

a savings pot for women in the UK of £69k, Kevin Peachy, BBC Correspondent, *Pension income needed to retire jumps as family costs rise* (2024), https://www.bbc.co.uk/news/business-68222807.

Chapter 6: About Your Health and Wellbeing

in a survey of Danish women, 62% confirmed a stronger sense of wellbeing, L Hvas, *Positive aspects of menopause: a qualitative study* (2001), Maturitas, https://pubmed.ncbi.nlm.nih.gov/11451616/.

65% of British women were happier, Social Issues Research Centre, *Jubilee Women, Fiftysomething Women – Lifestyle and Attitudes Now and Fifty Years Ago* (2023), http://www.sirc.org/publik/jubilee_women.pdf.

your brain neurons are mostly irreplaceable, National Research Council, *Shaping the Future: Biology and Human Values* (1989), Washington, D.C.: The National Academies Press, https://www.ncbi.nlm.nih.gov/books/NBK218597.

the natural tranquiliser of the nervous system, Dr Andrew Neil, https://www.drweil.com/videos-features/videos/the-4-7-8-breath-health-benefits-demonstration/.

visualisation mindfulness has its roots in Buddhism, https://buddhaweekly.com/visualization-activates-mind-mindfulness-stills-mind-right-buddhist-practice/.

Other health benefits reported, include a reduction in anxiety and depression, Rebecca Strong, *7 Health Benefits of Journaling and How to Make It an Effective Habit* (2022), https://www.businessinsider.com/guides/health/mental-health/benefits-of-journaling.

balance on one leg for at least 10 seconds, *Just one thing – with Michael Mosley: Stand on One Leg*, https://www.bbc.co.uk/programmes/articles/35QytBYmkXJ4JnDYl9zYngb/why-you-should-stand-on-one-leg.

35% had a lower risk of developing dementia, Annie Lennon, *New study investigates which activities are tied to a lower dementia risk* (2022), Medical News Today, https://www.medicalnewstoday.com/articles/new-study-investigates-which-activities-are-tied-to-a-lower-dementia-risk.

high intensity training, the opposite is true of women, Dr Lisa Mosconi, *The Menopause Brain* (2024), Pg 178, Allen & Unwin.

the habit loop, Charles Duhigg, *The Power of Habit: Why we do what we do in life and business* (2012), Penguin Books.

Chapter 7: Your Life Beyond the 9 to 5

Listening Skills Quiz – adapted from Deb Peterson, *Listening Test – Are You a Good Listener?* (2024), ThoughtCo, https://www.thoughtco.com/listening-test-are-you-a-good-listener-31656.

APPENDIX 1
RESEARCH INTERVIEW QUESTIONNAIRE

Name:	Age Now: *(Optional)*
	Age Wish to Retire:

Employment Status:	Professional Status:
□ Full-time Employment □ Part-time Employment □ Partially Retired □ Fully Retired □ Other	□ Employee □ Independent Contractor □ Business Owner □ Student/Apprentice □ Other

Generational Group:	Glidepath Years:*
□ Generation Z : Born 1997 – 2012 □ Millennial : Born 1980 – 1996 □ Generation X : Born 1965 - 1979 □ Baby Boomer : Born 1946 - 1964 □ Traditionalist : Born 1925 - 1945	□ More than 10 Years □ Between 5 and 10 Years □ Below 5 Years □ Within a Year

*The number of years from preferred retirement age** (or legal retirement age where applicable).*
**Also described below as the designated date.*

Q1. What retirement Savings have you in place?	☐ None ☐ I am in a Company sponsored Plan ☐ I have my own Personal Plan ☐ I have both a Company and a Personal Plan
Q2. Approximately what percentage of your gross pay are you currently contributing?	☐ None ☐ Less than 5% ☐ Between 5 and 10% ☐ Greater than 10%
Q3. Approximately what percentage of your pay is your company currently contributing?	☐ None ☐ Less than 5% ☐ Between 5 and 10% ☐ Greater than 10%
Q4. Do you believe you will have sufficient funds to be able to retire at your designated date? **Or, if your designated date has passed, did you have sufficient funds?**	☐ Yes ☐ No ☐ Maybe ☐ Don't Know

If no, are you able to share what you will do to bridge any gaps?

Or, if your designated date has passed, can you share what contingencies you have put in place to make ends meet?

Q5. What would be your ideal glidepath to your designated date?

Or, if your designated date has passed, what was your glidepath to your designated date?

- ☐ Work Full Time or your current hours if less
- ☐ Reduce working time gradually over the preceding 5 years
- ☐ Reduce working time gradually over the preceding 4 years
- ☐ Reduce working time gradually over the preceding 3 years
- ☐ Reduce working time gradually over the preceding 2 years
- ☐ Reduce working time only in last year
- ☐ Other

If 'Other', please explain.

Q6. From the following, choose what you consider the most likely affordability scenario for your projected or realised retirement assets:

	Property Care	Eat Out per Month	Transport	Holiday Abroad	Holiday at Home
☐	Minimal DIY	x1	No car	None	x1 week
☐	Some Decorating each year	x2	Replace every 7 years	1 x Fortnight (3 star)	x1 long weekend
☐	New Kitchen / Bathroom every 10 years	x3-4	Replace every 3 years	1 x Fortnight (4 star+)	x3 long weekends

Q7. What tips or suggestions would you be willing to share that could benefit others?

Q8. What support, if any, would you like to see Employing Organisations provide for people on their glidepath as standard?

Please tick all that apply:

☐ Flexibility in Working Hours
☐ Flexibility in Role and Responsibilities
☐ Structured Succession Planning
☐ Education on Retirement Planning
☐ Alumni for Retirees
☐ Other

If Other, please explain.

Q9. What support, if any, would you like to see State/Government departments officially introduce for people on their glidepath?

Q10. What, if anything, would you now change about your approach to your designated date?